Re-examining the UK Newspaper Industry

This book dispels myths surrounding the newspaper industry's financial viability in an online world, arguing that widespread predictions of pending newspaper extinction are based mostly on misunderstandings of the industry's operations.

Drawing from his training as a business journalist, Marc Edge undertakes a thorough analysis of annual financial statements provided by newspaper companies themselves to explain the industry's arcane economics. This book contextualises available data within the historical context in which various news publishers operate and outlines the economic history of UK newspapers. It also investigates how UK newspapers survived the 2008–09 recession, considering both national and provincial markets separately.

A rigorous look at an often-neglected aspect of the newspaper industry, this volume will be an essential read for scholars of media studies, journalism studies, and communication studies, especially those interested in studying journalism and news production as occupational identities.

Marc Edge was a newspaper journalist for twenty years in his native Canada, holding senior positions as an editor and reporter at the *Calgary Herald* and Vancouver *Province*. He studied for his doctorate in the E.W. Scripps School of Journalism at Ohio University, USA. He is the author of five previous books including *Greatly Exaggerated: The Myth of the Death of Newspapers* (2014).

Routledge Focus on Journalism Studies

Re-examining the UK Newspaper Industry

Marc Edge

NEW YORK AND LONDON

First published 2022
by Routledge
4 Park Square, Milton Park, Abingdon, Oxon OX14 4RN

and by Routledge
605 Third Avenue, New York, NY 10158

Routledge is an imprint of the Taylor & Francis Group, an informa business

© 2023 Taylor & Francis

British Library Cataloguing-in-Publication Data
A catalogue record for this book is available from the British Library

ISBN: 978-1-138-60305-9 (hbk)
ISBN: 978-1-032-39035-2 (pbk)
ISBN: 978-0-429-46920-6 (ebk)

DOI: 10.4324/9780429469206

Typeset in Times New Roman
by Apex Covantage, LLC

Contents

Preface

The falling fortunes of newspapers in the 21st century have led to much concern, but from researching the subject for more than a decade, I am convinced that the apprehension is largely unfounded. I love newspapers as much as anyone. I delivered the *Vancouver Sun* door-to-door as a lad in my native Canada, where I went on to a twenty-year career as a reporter and sub-editor on major metropolitan dailies. My research as a scholar over the past quarter century has focused on the business side of newspapers and has been greatly aided by my first two degrees in that field. What really opened my eyes, however, was a 2011 fellowship to the Reynolds Center for Business Journalism at Arizona State University, which included training in reading financial statements. I was almost ashamed to admit that I had already written two books on newspaper companies and scarcely glanced at an annual report.

I began to download and analyse media company financial statements for two academic journal articles I was then revising. What I found ran so counter to the dominant narrative on media fortunes that I actually reversed my conclusions in one of the articles. I then set to work on my 2014 book *Greatly Exaggerated: The Myth of the Death of Newspapers* (Vancouver: New Star Books). It found that no publicly traded newspaper company in North America suffered an annual loss on an operating basis between 2006 and 2013 despite their revenues dropping by about half in the United States and a quarter in Canada as a result of the 2008–09 recession. Newspapers were highly scalable, I concluded, and can cut their costs almost as rapidly as their revenues fall, unfortunately by mostly making journalists redundant.

My study of North American newspapers was limited to publicly traded companies, however, because privately owned firms here are not required to disclose their finances. In the United Kingdom, on the other hand, all incorporated entities must file annual financial statements with Companies House, including holding companies and subsidiaries. This has allowed for a fairly granular portrait to be drawn of newspaper fortunes there, as the data gathered by Companies House arguably exceed 100 percent coverage. For example, I could not untangle for *Greatly Exaggerated* the US newspapers owned by Rupert Murdoch's News Corp from its Australian and UK titles because they were lumped together in its financial statements as a division which also included its book publishing companies. In the United Kingdom, however, both Times Newspapers and News Group Newspapers, the latter of which publishes the *Sun*, are subsidiaries which must file separate financials with Companies House. Their annual reports are fairly forthcoming, unlike those of some publishers, and clearly state their earnings before interest, taxes, depreciation, and amortisation (EBITDA), which is generally considered to be the best measure of a company's financial performance.

Most companies instead report a version of operating profit, so digging into the footnotes of their financial statements is usually required to calculate EBITDA. Some publishers seem to obscure their finances as much as possible. Newsquest, for example, was until recently made up of dozens of subsidiaries which together published more than 300 newspapers, each of which filed its own financial statements with Companies House, so much work would be required to piece together a picture of the company's fortunes. Only once did Newsquest report its finances for the group as a whole, and that resulted in strikes and protests across the country in 2015 when they showed that the company made a huge profit off its mass layoff of workers the previous year, much of which went in bonuses to executives and directors (see Chapter 5). History repeated itself to a certain extent in 2022, when Newsquest Media Group Limited, the subsidiary into which Newsquest had by then folded most of its titles, filed its 2021 report with Companies House. It showed that its EBITDA had increased by 10 percent from 2020 to £35.6 million and its profit margin (return on revenue) by 2 percentage points to 25.1 percent, largely as a result of an 18-percent staff reduction. A spokesman for the National Union of Journalists (NUJ) accused the company of 'exporting' profits to its US parent chain Gannett in the form of a £15-million dividend (Tobbitt, 2022, 8 June).

Then there was the 2012 ruling by a tax tribunal which found that Iliffe Media, then one of the largest UK regional newspaper chains, had hidden millions of pounds from its reported earnings in order to reduce union wage demands and deter rivals from launching competing titles. Under the scheme, noted *Press Gazette*, millions of pounds were 'siphoned off from Iliffe's various local limited companies to appear in the accounts as "publishing rights and amortisation"' (Ponsford, 2012, 28 November). The deception came to the attention of tax authorities, and a tribunal ruled Iliffe Media liable to pay tax on £51.4 million of claimed deductions. On the whole, however, the reports available for download on the Companies House website have enabled UK journalists to report fairly accurately on the fortunes of their own industry, unlike in North America where myth and misinformation seem to hold the upper hand.

Since the outlook for the UK newspaper industry has come into question recently with a spate of inquiries and calls for Google and Facebook to help fund it, I felt that a study of company finances was in order. This book began as a paper delivered to the 2017 conference of the European Media Management Association in Ghent which was published in the *Journal of Media Business Studies* in 2019. The manuscript I promised to Routledge Research was delayed when I contracted COVID-19 in early 2020 and further delayed by my departure from the University of Malta later that year as a result of the pandemic and my relocation back home to Canada. COVID-19 caused such a disruption for newspapers that I felt the book should be put on hold until the dust settled, but by the second year of the pandemic their survival seemed all but assured by their rising profits, some of which were the best in years. Just how well newspapers ultimately weather the storm is still to be seen, but I hope that this book will contribute to the debate over the future of UK newspapers and to the deliberations by the latest Digital, Culture, Media and Sport (DCMS) inquiry into the sustainability of local journalism.

After this book was written and about to go into production, however, a report commissioned by DCMS for its inquiry was released, and it reached quite different conclusions from mine. While the report by consultancy Economic Insight (2022) contains some valuable information, including data on rising cover prices, industry liabilities, and cost-cutting measures being considered, I believe it is fundamentally flawed for several reasons. Most notable are its focus on hard copy sales and its promotion of equity investment as a solution. While print does still account for the bulk of newspaper revenues, it also accounts for the bulk of their costs. Since newspapers have historically been sold at a loss compared to their cost of production, publishers can actually save money by cutting back on circulation. They would much rather sell a digital subscription, which involves zero marginal cost, than print and deliver another hard copy, on which they lose money. Equity investment in newspapers, at least in North America where it dominates the industry, has been disastrous for news coverage due to its focus on profits ahead of journalism.

The report's data on digital subscriptions, which date to 2018, are also questionable. Economic Insight put the value of national newspaper online subscriptions that year at only £18 million, but the *Times* and *Sunday Times* passed 250,000 subscribers in 2018, the *Financial Times* had more than 700,000, and the *Telegraph* announced in 2019 that more than half of its

420,000 subscribers were digital. These numbers, as will be seen, have grown considerably in the four years since. Economic Insight examined Companies House filings, as I did, but again only as far as 2018 for some reason. Its report uses measures of profitability including Return on Assets, which depends entirely on how those assets are valued, and Return on Capital Employed. It emphasises the importance of capital expenditures, but the newspaper business has become much less capital intensive since the introduction of computer technology. In my experience, studies by economists of the newspaper business should always be balanced by the views of scholars from other fields in order to gain a more holistic understanding of this unique enterprise (Edge, 2020). Most of all, a focus on their bottom lines always seems to provide more insight into newspaper fortunes than how they or anybody else portray them.

One observable effect of the pandemic has been to accelerate changes that were already under way in society as a result of digital technology, such as e-commerce, remote working, and online news consumption. The latter will be vital for newspapers if they are to make the leap to profitable digital publications. Whether they will continue to also publish in hard copy is another matter, but they would have little incentive to mothball their presses as long as print advertising is profitable. That is why I believe that keeping an eye on their finances holds the key to predicting the future of newspapers. The vast store of longitudinal data available in Companies House filings should be given more attention by scholars studying newspapers and their ongoing transition to digital publications.

I would like to thank Suzanne Richardson, the commissioning editor for Media, Cultural and Communication Studies at Routledge Research and her predecessor, Felisa Salvago-Keyes, for believing in this project and for granting me so many extensions, along with Margaret Farrelly, who first saw the value in it. I would also like to thank editor Vaishnavi Madhavan and editorial assistants Tanushree Baijal and Richa Kohli for their help. Special thanks must go to Rachel Matthews of Coventry University, who was one of the first to encourage my research and also helped me to navigate some unfamiliar terrain, as did Gillian Doyle of the University of Glasgow and Andy Williams of Cardiff University. Credit should also be given to Tom Evens of Ghent University for rescuing my original EMMA paper proposal from among the rejects on appeal. Any errors or omissions, of course, are purely my own.

Ladysmith, British Columbia
July 2022

Introduction

A Pandemic Stress Test

The newspaper industry was already considered beleaguered when the COVID-19 pandemic began in 2020, and the economic and social disruption it soon brought threatened to finish them off. Predictions had been made for decades that new media would kill printed news. First it was radio in the 1920s, then television in the 1950s, and finally the Internet in the 1990s, but newspapers proved adaptable and resilient. By the early years of the 21st century, most were highly profitable. National newspapers no longer sold millions of copies a day, but copy sales were never what drove their profits. Advertising was what had filled the coffers of press barons from the days of Northcliffe and Kemsley, and with the rise of mass marketing it grew after World War II into a long-lived bubble. In the Internet age, however, websites began to siphon off their rich advertising revenues. Classified ads were the first to go, as specialised sites for homes, autos, and situations vacant offered sortable databases of listings for house hunters, car buyers, and job seekers. Then the so-called Great Recession of 2008–09, the longest and deepest since the 1930s, crashed the economy and burst the advertising bubble. Some advertisers never returned to newspapers even after the economy recovered, having found cheaper alternatives online.

The online advertising alternatives were not just cheaper but also more effective. The classic complaint of newspaper advertisers was articulated by Unilever founder Lord Leverhulme more than a century ago when he said: 'Half the money I spend on advertising is wasted, and the trouble is I don't know which half' (Barrett, 2010). The ability of websites to follow users around online with pieces of code embedded in their browsers called 'cookies' allowed them to gather vast amounts of data. This enabled the perfection of target marketing and ushered in an era of 'surveillance capitalism'. Google proved the master at this, pairing the data it compiled on users of its popular search engine with its AdSense online ad sales business. Facebook wasn't far behind, using the data it gathered on members of its

DOI: 10.4324/9780429469206-1

social network to sell ads tailored to their interests. The digital advertising which newspapers hoped would flow to their online editions to replace the print ads they had lost instead went mostly to Google and Facebook. Most publishers in fact used Google's AdSense programme on their own web pages because it was so effective.

Then the pandemic hit in March 2020. Advertising dried up as business ground to a halt. Commuters stayed home and shops shuttered as lockdowns were ordered to cope with successive variants of the virus. Newsstand sales plummeted as a result. Newspapers responded by making workers redundant. The giant chain Reach plc furloughed a fifth of its 4,700 staff that April under the government's coronavirus job retention scheme, which paid 80 percent of their wages. It also cut the pay of its remaining staff by 10 percent for three months, with senior managers taking a 20-percent cut (Linford, 2020). Expecting its revenues to drop by 10 percent, or £20 million, the *Guardian* furloughed 100 staff (Anonymous, 2020). Newspaper publishers across the country furloughed hundreds of journalists (Sharman, 2020, 3 April). The Wolverhampton-based Midland News Association, which published the *Express & Star* and *Shropshire Star* regional dailies along with sixteen weeklies, furloughed more than 230 workers, or 29 percent of its staff (Sharman, 2021, 6 January). The independent *South London Press* placed half its team of 12 on furlough and published an appeal to readers for donations (Sharman, 2020, 15 April).

Reach, which had recently changed its name from Trinity Mirror to signify its growing size, was the largest UK chain with approximately a fifth of both the national and provincial newspaper markets. It was also one of the few publicly traded chains, and it was thus required to report its finances quarterly for the benefit of investors. Its announcement in July 2020 suggested the scale of the pandemic's effect on the press. With its second-quarter revenues down by 27.5 percent, Reach made 550 workers redundant, or about 12 percent of its workforce, including about 325 in editorial and circulation. The permanent job cuts were designed to save Reach £35 million a year, and they cost it £16.5 million in severance payments (Sharman, 2020, 7 July). Long-time *Guardian* media columnist Roy Greenslade (2020) warned that the pandemic would 'likely mark the final stage in newsprint's long decline'.

> Coronavirus is destroying newsprint newspapers across Britain, delivering the coup de grace to businesses that were already in the process of dying. There will not be a post-pandemic 'old media' recovery because it seems inconceivable that publishers, already struggling to fund journalism, will return to the previous status quo.
>
> (Greenslade, 2020)

Ironically, however, newspapers had more readers than ever despite their plummeting print sales as people increasingly went online for news during the pandemic. Traffic to the *Financial Times* website, which dropped its paywall for COVID-19 news, surged 250 percent. Mirror.co.uk saw a 60-percent increase, while the number of unique visitors to the *Guardian*'s website almost doubled (Mayhew, 2020). It was a phenomenon that had been noticed for years. As their print circulation went down, newspapers gained readers online. The problem was that their online readers were mostly free riders, as British newspapers largely hesitated to charge readers for access to their online content for fear of losing traffic and thus ad revenue, but increasingly ads were eluding them. Allowing free online access to their content had been called the 'original sin' of newspapers in the Internet age (Mutter, 2009). The *Financial Times* introduced a paywall in 2007, however, that was designed to maximise revenue from both online ads and online subscriptions. It allowed readers a number of free articles every month, thus letting most traffic through, before asking regular readers to subscribe in what was called a 'metered' paywall. It worked so well that Japanese publisher Nikkei paid £844 million for the *FT* in 2015. The metered paywall was also adopted by the *New York Times* in 2011, and it proved so successful that by 2018 it had more than 2.6 million digital subscribers paying more than US$1 billion a year (Bond, 2018). With the pandemic, its subscriptions rose to more than 7.5 million (Tracy, 2021). Most UK publishers were reluctant to put their online content behind a paywall, however. One reason was the lack of a subscription culture given that three-quarters of newspaper copy sales in the United Kingdom were made at newsstands, unlike in most other countries where they were mostly delivered to homes (Cairncross, 2019). A multi-country study by the Reuters Institute for the Study of Journalism at Oxford also found that the United Kingdom lagged in paywalls because of its highly competitive national newspaper market, in which leading titles feared losing market share (Simon & Graves, 2019).

One paywall adopter was News UK, whose owner Rupert Murdoch ordered a 'hard' paywall around the websites of its *Times* newspapers in 2010, with no free articles. Murdoch was an outsized figure who dominated the media not just in the United Kingdom but globally. He was considered by some to be the world's most powerful man for his media holdings, which he often used for political purposes (Kitty, 2005). Murdoch served as the template for a literal Bond villain in 1997's 'Tomorrow Never Dies', and his family's corporate machinations inspired the HBO series 'Succession'. According to a book by two reporters for the *New York Times*, US president Joe Biden referred to Murdoch as 'the most dangerous man in the world' and to his Fox News television network as 'one of the most destructive forces in the United States' (Martin & Burns, 2022, p. 354). Murdoch was just as reviled in the United Kingdom, where he bought the *Sun* broadsheet in 1969 and turned it into a sensational tabloid which pictured a topless model daily on page 3 and became Britain's best-selling newspaper. After he bought the *Times* in 1981, Murdoch broke the powerful newspaper unions by moving out of Fleet Street under massive police protection to non-union premises at Wapping. The savings in labour and printing costs were enormous and helped to fund Murdoch's expansion to America, where his New York-based media conglomerate News Corp owned two TV networks and several major dailies, including the *New York Post* and the *Wall Street Journal*.

Its subsidiary News Corp UK & Ireland Limited, which was usually shortened to News UK, published almost a third of Britain's national newspaper circulation in the *Times*, *Sunday Times, Sun*, and *Sun on Sunday*. It closed its *News of the World* in 2011, however, after a phone-hacking scandal revealed it had intercepted the private conversations of celebrities, crime victims, and even royals, resulting in the Leveson inquiry into newspaper ethics. Victims group Hacked Off, headed by actor Hugh Grant, campaigned for media regulation. The select committee of the Digital, Culture, Media and Sport (DCMS) ministry then deemed Murdoch 'not a fit person' to head a major international company and News Corp withdrew its bid for control of the BSkyB satellite broadcaster (Sabbagh & Halliday, 2012). Murdoch was known for bold moves, most of which proved his genius, but no other UK newspaper publisher joined him in erecting a hard paywall. Few other than the *Financial Times* and the *Telegraph* bothered with a paywall of any kind, and they kept changing theirs. Online subscription schemes were unpredictable and not always profitable. News UK had to drop the paywall around the website of its *Sun*, for example, after few paid to read it online.

Another strategy Murdoch used was to push for Google and Facebook to pay publishers for news stories they linked to, claiming the digital platforms were stealing their content. He once called Google a 'content kleptomaniac' and threatened to licence his company's articles to Microsoft's rival search engine Bing (Gapper, 2009). In early 2010, News UK blocked the aggregator NewsNow, which offered a paid service to subscribers, from linking to content from its websites (Bunz, 2010). The social network MySpace, which Murdoch bought in 2005 for £304 million, briefly partnered with Google in an ad deal until MySpace was surpassed in popularity first by Bebo and then by Facebook (van Duyn & Waters, 2006).

Murdoch didn't hesitate to use his media holdings in waging his battle with the digital giants. The *Times* conducted a month-long campaign against the platforms in 2017, noted Buzzfeed, including 18 front-page stories on Facebook and Google. 'They aren't afraid to use their own media properties as weapons. Which isn't to say that reporters are directly told to go after Facebook or Google, but that those stories are prioritized' (Perlberg & Di Stefano, 2017). Murdoch had good reason to play up any negative news about the tech platforms, it noted, as News Corp had invested in a rival to Google's DoubleClick ad-matching service called AppNexus and planned its own digital advertising network (Perlberg & Di Stefano, 2017). Murdoch's campaign against Google and Facebook gained traction first in Australia, where he owned 14 of the country's 21 metropolitan daily and Sunday newspapers (Flew, 2013). As the pandemic began, the government there ordered legislation that would force the digital platforms to share their revenues with news media. Facebook responded by threatening to ban links to Australian news stories from its pages. The backlash against Murdoch down under showed he was just as reviled in his own country as elsewhere. Former Australian Prime Minister Kevin Rudd launched a petition in late 2020 demanding a royal commission into his media influence, calling Murdoch 'an arrogant cancer on our democracy' (Galloway, 2020). It soon gained more than a half million signatures and the support of fellow former Prime Minister Malcolm Turnbull (Thorpe & Meade, 2020). Rudd claimed that Murdoch's dominance of the country's media, which also included Sky News Australia, had created a 'culture of fear' (Simons, 2020).

The campaign against Google and Facebook in the United Kingdom was led by *Press Gazette*, which had covered the news business as a magazine since 1965 before going online-only in 2013. It began its Duopoly campaign in early 2017 to stop Google and Facebook from what it called 'destroying' journalism. 'Imagine if two news publishers dominated digital media in the way that Facebook and Google do', it asked. 'The Government would not allow such a duopoly to stand. Campaigners would call for them to be broken up in the name of media plurality' (Ponsford, 2017, 10 April). *Press Gazette* launched a petition urging Google and Facebook to 'return more value' to the news industry (Ponsford, 2017, 10 April).

A series of government inquiries ensued, the likes of which had not been seen since a trilogy of royal commissions into the press in the three decades following World War II. First, however, the government cancelled a planned second stage of the Leveson phone-hacking inquiry that was to examine relations between press and police in 2018. Culture Secretary Matt Hancock told the House of Commons that the press was under threat from new forces which required urgent attention, and that local papers in particular were under 'severe' pressure. 'Newspaper circulation has fallen by around 30 per cent since the conclusion of the Leveson Inquiry', Hancock noted, citing statistics which showed that for every £100 newspapers lost in print revenue in 2015, they gained only £3 in digital revenue. 'We do not believe that this costly and time-consuming public inquiry is the right way forward' (Hancock, 2018). He also cancelled a planned new Section 40 of the Crime and Courts Act, which would have forced newspapers not under an approved regulator to pay the legal fees of parties suing them whether they won or not, saying it would 'exacerbate the problems the press face rather than solve them' (Hancock, 2018). Hancock added that Britain needed 'high-quality journalism to thrive in the new digital world', and the following month he announced an inquiry into just that. Declaring that the Internet had 'torn apart the established order and raised real questions about the sustainability and profitability of traditional journalism', he appointed Dame Frances Cairncross, a former journalist for the *Economist* and the *Guardian*, to examine the sustainability of high-quality UK journalism.

The Cairncross Review received submissions that called for government subsidies to the press, such as Canada had recently announced as part of a five-year C$595 million (£330 million) bailout, and others which called for Google and Facebook to contribute a portion of their revenues. The NUJ suggested 'an economic stimulus plan for the media including arms-length government subsidies' (Tobitt, 2018, 25 September). The newspaper industry group News Media Association (NMA) asked the government to make Facebook and Google pay an annual levy to fund journalism, noting that they made 'no meaningful contribution to the cost of producing the original content from which they so richly benefit'. Its submission also called for tax credits which would allow newspapers to claim a cash rebate for investment in journalism, similar to what Canada had recently announced (Waterson, 2018). Cairncross, however, noted 'surprising' evidence that most UK newspapers remained comfortably profitable and declined to recommend direct government funding or a forced redistribution of profits from Google and Facebook.

> In making the case for intervention in support of journalism, it is important at the outset to acknowledge . . . that most national newspapers and regional newspaper groups are generating good profits, with margins of 10 percent or more.
>
> (Cairncross, 2019, p. 14)

Her report issued in early 2019 noted that both platforms had recently undertaken to help improve digital newsgathering, with a Facebook Journalism Project pledging £4.5 million to fund training for 80 new community journalists and a Google News Initiative awarding £10.5 million to publishers across 66 projects. The Cairncross report urged only that a watching brief be kept on the digital giants while helping publishers to become self-sufficient, including with a government innovation fund. The resulting £2 million Future News Fund set up as a one-year pilot project, however, fell far short of the £10 million a year over four years recommended by Cairncross (Granger, 2019). After funding 19 small publishers, it was reconstituted as the independent charity Public Interest News Foundation due to concerns over 'perceptions of inappropriate government interference with the press' (Granger, 2020).

A month after the Cairncross report was released, a report on competition in the digital age commissioned by the Chancellor of the Exchequer found UK merger and antitrust laws inadequate to counter the market dominance of Google and Facebook. It proposed the establishment of a new body to draw up a code of competitive conduct to which they would have to adhere, which led to creation of a new Digital Markets Unit (Hern, 2020). Still the government inquiries continued. A House of Lords report on the future of UK journalism urged in late 2020 that the government enact a mandatory news bargaining code based on the Australian model to be supervised by the new DMU (House of Lords, 2020).

By 2021, however, the financial fortunes of the UK press had made a dramatic recovery despite the ongoing pandemic. Some newspapers reimbursed the government for furlough payments, including the *Telegraph* and the *Guardian*, while others, such as the *Times* and *Daily Mail*, never used the scheme (Tobitt, 2021, 10 August). Reach announced early in the year that it expected to declare a 2020 profit of between £130 million and £135 million due to its record digital performance. While its print sales were down about 12 percent in the second half of the year, its digital revenue had increased by 13.4 percent in the third quarter and almost 25 percent in quarter four (Sharman, 2021, 8 January). Reach even agreed to repay the £4 million it had saved from staff pay cuts, but not before a group of its workers lodged an employment tribunal claim for unlawful deduction of wages (Tobitt, 2021, 19 April). By mid-year, the company's finances looked even better, as it announced that thanks to strong growth in digital advertising its profit for the first six months of 2021 was £68 million and its profit margin had increased from 19 percent to 23 percent (Tobitt, 2021, 27 July).

Soon newspapers across the country were hiring again after one study found a 17.9 percent surge in local news readership online in 2021. The increase was led by young people, who had previously been notorious for paying little attention to local news, with readership among the 15–34 age group increasing 18.5 percent (Sharman, 2021, 28 October). Reach began recruiting more than 300 new digital journalists due to the success of its registration scheme, under which online readers had to provide data such as their email address or postcode (Nilsson, 2021). Newsquest, the largest chain of local and regional newspapers, also began hiring after its online readership rose by 40 percent in 2020. Owned by the largest US chain Gannett, which had recently been taken over by a hedge fund, Newsquest also began erecting paywalls at more of its newspapers, going from only about five out of 160 titles to about 65 (Nilsson, 2021). Archant, the fourth largest provincial chain, began looking for 70 new employees and JPIMedia, which had recently taken over third-largest chain Johnston Press, started recruiting 45 staff for new digital titles it planned across the country (Sharman, 2021, 7 December).

Press Gazette calculated the market capitalisation of listed publishers that fall and declared the chains had made a 'full comeback' (Turvill, 2021). By multiplying their number of issued shares by their current price, it found that all were worth more than before the pandemic, some several times more. New York-based News Corp's market cap fell from more than US$8 billion to around US$5 billion as the pandemic began, but it had rebounded to about US$14 billion. Reach's had dropped from £400 million to less than £200 million but had since climbed to more than £1 billion. Daily Mail and General Trust (DMGT), which published the commuter tabloids *i* and *Metro* in addition to its *Mail* titles, saw its market cap fall from £1.7 billion to around £1.4 billion, but it had then risen to more than £2 billion (Turvill, 2021). The annual digital media report of the Reuters Institute found that 59 percent of news company chief executives, editors, and other managers reported that their revenues increased in 2021, with only 8 percent reporting a drop (Newman, 2022).

One indicator of the newfound press prosperity came in early 2022 when Reach (2022) released its 2021 annual report, which showed that its operating profit had risen to £146 million.[1] It also revealed that the remuneration of its top executives, including incentives, had risen by 700 percent that year, including an increase for its CEO from £485,000 to £4.089 million (Kersley, 2022). *Press Gazette* investigated and found that DMGT paid its top executives even more in 2021, with its CEO making £9.72 million and its chief financial officer £6.6 million. DMGT chairman Lord Rothermere exceeded even that, grossing £10.91 million, an increase of almost half from the £7.34 million he was paid in 2020 (Kersley, 2022). The 4th Viscount Rothermere, who had been born Jonathan Harmsworth, was the great-grandson of company founder Harold Harmsworth and the largest DMGT shareholder with 37 percent of its stock. In late 2021, he bought out other shareholders at a reported cost of £3 billion and announced he would de-list DMGT from the London Stock Exchange and take the company private (Tobitt, 2021, 3 November).

Newspapers were simply picking up where they had left off when the pandemic struck. Quietly, amid all the official inquiries and fears for their future, newspapers had grown more prosperous than they had been in years. A decade on from the economic shock of the 2008–09 recession, they seemed to be finally coming to grips with the disruption to their business model caused by the Internet. The national newspapers each seemed to be finding their own way differently to profitability in the brave new online world. The *Daily Mail* kept its website free, and by focusing heavily on celebrity news and other clickbait, or what its online editor called 'journalism crack', it passed the *New York Times* in 2011 as the most widely read English language news website in the world (Bloomgarden-Smoke, 2014). Despite being a listed company, DMGT's quarterly and annual reports did not separate the finances of its newspaper division DMG Media from its corporate events, property information, and venture capital businesses. As a subsidiary, however, DMG Media had to file annual financial statements with corporate regulator Companies House under its original name of Associated Newspapers. They showed that it recorded an operating profit of £64.9 million and a profit margin of 13.7 percent in its fiscal year ended 30 September 2020. Its 2020–21 financial report was not filed with Companies House after more than a year, but parent company DMGT's annual report stated that revenues for its DMG Media division increased by 3 percent that year and its cash operating income rose by 7 percent to £69 million, for an 11 percent profit margin.

News UK could thank its hard paywall for helping its subsidiary Times Newspapers almost double its earnings in the company's fiscal year ended 30 June 2020 to £26.3 million. Operating profits at the *Telegraph* rose 25 percent to £40.4 million in 2021 as its digital subscription revenues grew by 40 percent to £44.1 million. It had 577,720 subscribers to its premium online content, it announced, and seven million registered readers of its free online content (Telegraph Media Group, 2022). Even the *Guardian*, which had lost tens of millions of pounds a year for almost a decade, made money in 2021 after simply asking its readers to contribute voluntarily. The *Guardian* not only kept its website free but also continued to provide quality journalism in quantity, as it was underwritten by the rich Scott Trust. The *Guardian* lost a company record £68.7 million in 2016, however, which threatened to quickly drain its nest egg, but in early 2017 it announced that since making its appeal it had gained 200,000 paying 'members' and that a further 160,000 readers had made one-time donations (Ponsford, 2017, 17 March). By its fiscal year ended 31 March 2020, Guardian Media Group plc had cut its annual loss to £6.9 million. In November 2021, it announced that it had more than 1 million paying readers in 180 countries and it recorded a profit of £12.4 million that year, its first in more than a decade. Its 2021-22 profit would reach £20.7 million (see Chapter 4).

Profits in the provincial press were also robust, contrary to public and even official perceptions. Its annual financial statements to Companies House showed that Newsquest Media Group Limited recorded earnings of £35.6 million in 2021 and its profit margin rose to 25.1 percent. Reach Regionals Media Limited saw its earnings increase for the second straight year to £30.3 million in 2021. Even JPIMedia, which was formed when Johnston Press went bankrupt in 2018 because of its enormous debt, made £12 million in 2021 at a profit margin of 13.9 percent. Johnston Press was a conundrum in that it was highly profitable at the time of its bankruptcy, with a profit margin above 20 percent from 2014 until 2017, when it slipped to 19.9 percent (see Chapter 5).

Some publishers were making more money than they had in years, according to Companies House filings. Aberdeen Journals Limited, which published the local dailies *Press and Journal* and *Evening Express*, along with the free weekly *Aberdeen Citizen*, had enjoyed profit margins in excess of 30 percent since 2014 which topped out in 2020 at 37.9 percent. Its owner, Dundee-based DC Thomson, was a private media conglomerate with holdings in books, magazines, broadcasting, comic books, and digital media. It also published Dundee's jointly operating *Courier* and *Evening Telegraph* dailies, along with the regional *Sunday Post*. DC Thomson's annual filings to Companies House did not break down its finances by division, but it bought Aberdeen Journals Limited from DMGT in 2006, so it had to file its results separately with Companies House because it was held as a subsidiary. Over a fifteen-year period, they showed the same pattern exhibited by most UK newspaper companies. The 2008–09 recession saw its revenues drop rapidly by almost 20 percent, and they continued to erode more slowly as advertising moved online. Its profits had largely recovered by 2014, however, as expressed by the standardised measure of earnings before interest, taxes, depreciation, and amortisation (EBITDA) (Table 0.1).

Table 0.1 Aberdeen Journals Limited

	Revenues (£m)	*EBITDA (£m)*	*Margin %*
2007	40.0	9.7	24.3
2008	40.0	9.7	24.3
2009	38.0	8.1	21.3
2010	32.5	4.5	13.8
2011	32.7	4.7	14.4
2012	32.2	5.0	15.5
2013	31.7	6.3	19.9
2014	30.1	9.2	30.5
2015	29.5	9.3	31.5
2016	27.0	8.8	32.6
2017	25.9	9.0	34.7
2018	24.7	8.0	32.4
2019	24.3	8.2	33.7
2020	22.7	8.6	37.9
2021	18.4	5.8	31.5

Year ending 31 March
Source: Companies House filings

Cost-cutting and other efficiencies brought its earnings back to almost the level seen before the 2008–09 recession until the pandemic suddenly dropped its revenues again.

The turnaround came after DC Thomson put a metered paywall around the online content of its *Press and Journal* in 2014, allowing readers ten free articles a month before asking them to pay £10 for a monthly subscription (Turvill, 2014). Aberdeen Journals Limited's earnings and profit margin shot up by about half that year, and the gains continued into the pandemic. The *Press and Journal* paywall was so successful that DC Thomson erected one around its *Dundee Courier* in 2016, asking its readers to register after three articles a month and to start paying after ten (Ponsford, 2016). The fiscal year for DC Thomson and its subsidiaries ended on 31 March, so the 2020–21 annual report for Aberdeen Journals Limited allowed a glimpse into how its newspapers fared during a full pandemic year. While its revenues and earnings slumped with a downturn in sales, its profit margin remained above 30 percent. In early 2021, DC Thomson announced a recruitment drive to hire 20 journalists in order to boost its online content, including ten for a live news team (Tobitt, 2021, 27 January).

The Australian parliament introduced its promised legislation in late 2020 to force Google and Facebook to pay publishers when links to news stories appeared on their platforms. This prompted a standoff with Facebook, which for a day refused to carry links to news stories from that country. It relented after changes were made to the bill, which was enacted as the News Media and Digital Platforms Mandatory Bargaining Code. In early 2021, News Corp reached a three-year agreement with Google under which the publisher would receive an undisclosed but 'significant' payment for its stories featured in Google's News Showcase (James, 2021). While great secrecy surrounded the Australian digital payments, it was reported that News Corp Australia received at least A$70 million (£40 million) a year from Google and Facebook (Grueskin, 2022). In late 2021, the Australian Senate called for a judicial inquiry into media diversity, ownership, and regulation (Meade, 2021).

In the United Kingdom, yet another media inquiry was announced in early 2022, this one by DCMS into the sustainability of local journalism. Even as it gathered evidence, however, newspaper ownership contracted again, as Newsquest bought the fourth largest chain Archant that March. It published four regional dailies, including England's largest selling in the *Eastern Daily Press*, along with more than 60 paid and free weekly newspapers. It had gone into bankruptcy administration in 2020, but like Johnston Press it was also comfortably profitable. Archant's problem was its £114 million pension deficit. It agreed in 2017 to pay £3 million a year to reduce it but was unable to keep up the payments after the COVID-19 pandemic dropped its revenues. It was acquired out of administration by a London-based hedge fund, while its pension obligations were assumed by the Pension Protection Fund, which took 10-percent ownership of the company. Its subsequent purchase by Newsquest made it by far the largest owner of UK local and regional newspapers with more than 300.

The growing concentration of UK press ownership worried the Media Reform Coalition (MRC), a group of academics and activists headquartered at the University of London. Its takeover of Archant, it pointed out, gave Newsquest more than 30 percent of the local and regional newspaper markets. 'The three largest companies – Newsquest, Reach and JPI Media – jointly control almost 70 percent of all local newspaper circulation' (Media Reform Coalition, 2022). The MRC periodically recalculated media ownership concentration, and its 2021 report found that the number of national newspaper publishers had fallen since 2016 from nine to six with the *Independent*'s move to online-only publication, the sale of the Express group to Reach, and the sale of *i* to DMGT. 'Just three companies – DMG Media, News UK and Reach – dominate 90 percent of the national newspaper market, up from 83 percent in 2019' (Media Reform Coalition, 2021, p. 2). This level of concentration, it added, allowed media owners to 'amass huge political and economic power and distort the media landscape to suit their interests and personal views' (Media Reform Coalition, 2021, p. 2).

UK media ownership rules rarely prevented increased press consolidation. The 2002 Enterprise Act allowed the Secretary of State to block mergers and acquisitions which raised a public interest concern over plurality of media control, while the 2003 Communications Act limited newspaper ownership of Channel 3. Ofcom was charged with revisiting the rules every three years, and its latest reviews threatened to weaken them. Its 2018 report found that the growth in online news had 'the potential to strengthen plurality and reduce the influence of any one media owner' and questioned whether plurality 'might be less of a concern now' (Ofcom, 2018, p. 2). Noting that DMGT called Google and Facebook 'the most significant threat to media plurality in the UK', its 2021 review recommended that the Secretary of State broaden the public interest test in the Enterprise Act beyond print newspapers and broadcasters to also include online 'news creators' (Ofcom, 2021, p. 9).

The extent to which the improvement in newspaper fortunes since 2015 had escaped official notice was exemplified in early 2022 when then-Secretary of State Nadine Dorries released Murdoch from his long-standing pledge to keep the *Times* and *Sunday Times* separate. The undertaking had been in place since 1981, when Murdoch bought the papers, and had been intended to safeguard media plurality. As the first year of the pandemic was ending, however, News UK asked to be released from the expense of keeping the titles separate, including the salaries of six independent directors. 'The direct and indirect costs of maintaining the Undertakings in the current circumstances risks adversely impacting the quality of journalism at *The Times* and *The Sunday Times* and, ultimately, the economic viability of the two titles' (News Corp UK, 2021, p. 2). Its application pointed to the government's approval of the Northern & Shell takeover by Reach, which gave it the *Express* and *Star* daily and Sunday nationals in addition to its *Mirror* titles, and its green lighting of DMGT's purchase of the *i*. It noted the declining print circulation and advertising revenue of its *Times* papers but made no mention of their growing online revenues. The COVID-19 crisis, it claimed, had put publisher costs 'under further and unprecedented pressure, which is unlikely to abate in the short to medium term' (News Corp UK, 2021, p. 10). Dorries agreed that there had been a 'material change of circumstances' in the newspaper industry and lifted the restrictions after a consultation brought no objections (Tobitt, 2022). The 2020–21 annual report for Times Newspapers Limited filed with Companies House the following month, however, showed that its profits had doubled again to £52.5 million and that its profit margin had increased to 16 percent. Its revenues had risen by £17 million, or 5 percent, thanks to strong growth in digital advertising and subscription revenues, as well as cover price increases which more than offset declines in print circulation and advertising. Online subscriptions had grown by 31,000 in the previous twelve months to 367,000 and represented 63 percent of *Times* subscribers. Inclusion of its content in the Apple+ online news service had attracted younger readers, with women rising to 56 percent of subscribers from 50 percent in 2020.

Turning threats into opportunities is a basic business school technique, but the special pleadings of newspaper owners stretched the limits of selectivity. They had passed their pandemic stress test with aplomb and were making good profits, but still they pushed for regulatory largesse. Their campaign to persuade the government to force Google and Facebook to share their revenues with them looked more likely to succeed with each new inquiry as the Cairncross review's advice to follow the money seemed to have been forgotten.

This study hopes to remedy that omission with a comprehensive review of UK newspaper finances. It does so by examining the financial reports they are required by law to file with Companies House and putting those data into historical and theoretical context. It first looks into how newspapers survived the 2008–09 recession, then at the economic history of UK newspapers before considering the national and provincial markets separately, including an examination of their financial filings.

Note

1. For the purposes of standardisation, its EBITDA (earnings before interest, taxes, depreciation and amortisation) for 2021 has been calculated as $165.4 million after adding to operating profits amounts deducted for amortisation and depreciation (see Chapter 4).

1 A Digital Dark Age for Newspapers

Media analyst Claire Enders delivered a dire warning in June 2009. Growing use of the Internet and the ongoing recession, she told a Commons committee, would soon devastate one of the UK's most cherished institutions – the press. Newspapers would largely be a thing of the past within a very few years, she told MPs, especially the nation's local and regional press. 'The community titles are the ones that are most at risk', Enders testified to the Culture, Media and Sport (CMS) ministry committee as it held hearings on the future of local and regional media. 'We are expecting up to half of all the 1,300 titles will close in the next five years' (Brook, 2009). Enders, whose husband Christopher Thomson was the CEO of media conglomerate DC Thomson, added: 'Many titles are already running at losses and are being sustained by the good graces of their owners, and that may not last' (Brook, 2009). Websites had taken advertising revenue from newspapers even before the recession, and then the ad market collapsed with the global stock market crash in late 2008. Enders predicted that newspaper advertising revenues in the United Kingdom would drop by 52 percent – or £1.3 billion – between 2007 and 2013, meaning the bottom would effectively fall out of the business (Brook, 2009). Enders had made a similar warning the previous year, telling a conference in London that a third of the UK's regional newspapers, two national newspapers, and half of the jobs in regional media would disappear in the next five years (McNally, 2008).

Her prediction came with some credibility, as Enders was considered something of a seer when it came to media. Her claim to fame since founding Enders Analysis in 1997 had been predicting the dot-com collapse at the millennium. If she was right about that, she just might be right about newspapers, too. 'We're going to end up, not far ahead, with a very small number of national newspapers', she told a *Guardian* reporter who soon visited her Soho offices for an interview (Kirwan, 2009). The loss of 20,000 media jobs as a result of newspaper closures, she added, would bring 'a decline of

DOI: 10.4324/9780429469206-2

original content across the board that will have enormous consequences for democracy' (Kirwan, 2009). According to Alan Rusbridger, then editor of the *Guardian*, Enders predicted in a 2009 corporate presentation that seven national newspapers would close by 2014 as 80 percent of their readership and ad revenue vanished (Rusbridger, 2018). The possibility was plausible, Rusbridger admitted in his book *Breaking News*, since the Guardian Media Group (GMG) had just recorded an operating loss of £36.8 million as classified advertising walked out the door. 'The bleak truth was that nearly £40 million in revenue had simply disappeared in two years' (Rusbridger, 2018, p. 166).

Enders wasn't the first to predict the demise of newspapers, and she wouldn't be the last. The *Economist* magazine, which stubbornly referred to itself as a newspaper because that was how it started life in 1843, published an obituary for the medium in 2006, asking in ransom note letters on its cover: 'Who Killed the Newspaper?' Like most, it pointed to the Internet as a prime suspect. 'Even the most confident of newspaper bosses now agree that they will survive in the long term only if . . . they can reinvent themselves on the internet and on other new-media platforms' (Anonymous, 2006). In the United States, where the number of newspapers had been dropping steadily for decades, journalism professor Philip Meyer (2004) predicted precisely in his book *The Vanishing Newspaper* that due to a lack of readers the last copy would be printed in March 2043.

Publishers and journalists who appeared before the CMS committee demanded MPs do something to help. Johnston Press CEO John Fry testified that his chain's advertising revenues had dropped by 40 percent over the previous two years. Trinity Mirror had closed 35 of its 150 local newspapers in 2008 and 2009. The NUJ counted the closure of 60 local newspapers in the previous twelve months alone, with the loss of more than 1,500 jobs (House of Commons, 2010). Some of the industry's misery, the committee heard, was even of the government's making, such as the Royal Mail ending delivery of local papers.

The biggest blow, however, had been the placing of government advertising online. 'The government started to withdraw recruitment advertising from the local press in 2004 and that has been absolutely the most awful thing', testified Enders (Brook, 2009). The Scottish Daily Newspaper Society blamed a website operated by the Convention of Scottish Local Authorities for the loss of £13.5 million in local authority recruitment advertising. Governments had even started their own newspapers in competition with local titles, publishers noted. The Local Government Association launched a 'Reputation Campaign' in 2005 which encouraged local authorities to improve communications with residents by publishing their own council newspapers. Nearly all had done so by 2009, diverting public notice advertising away from the traditional press. Worse, the editorial content of council newspapers was hardly objective or independent, noted publishers, and often amounted to propaganda (House of Commons, 2010). Newspaper publishers wanted a stop put to the publicly funded competition. The industry also wanted a relaxation of government restrictions on newspaper consolidation, which Enders argued would be 'key to its survival, and uppermost in the strategies of publishers for the near future' (House of Commons, 2010, p. 19).

The newspaper crisis had already roiled the United States, where the closure in March 2009 of the long-publishing *Rocky Mountain News* in Denver and the exile to online-only publication of the *Seattle Post-Intelligencer* brought predictions of imminent newspaper extinction. Journalist and author Michael Wolff warned that 80 percent of newspapers would be gone within eighteen months (Kaplan, 2009). *Time* magazine agreed, predicting on its website: 'It's possible that eight of the nation's 50 largest daily newspapers could cease publication in the next 18 months' (McIntyre, 2009). Even the *New York Times* went on the endangered list after news broke that its parent company had lost US$74.5 million in the first quarter of 2009. The *Atlantic* magazine predicted that the *Times* could go out of business within months, noting that 'drastic measures will have to be taken over the next five months or the paper will default on some $400 million in debt' (Hirschorn, 2009). The economics of newspapers had been 'destroyed', according to New York University professor Clay Shirky (2009), because the Internet had provided a low-cost solution to the expensive problem of printing and distribution. 'There is no general model for newspapers to replace the one the internet just broke', he wrote on his blog. 'With the old economics destroyed, organizational forms perfected for industrial production have to be replaced with structures optimized for digital data' (Shirky, 2009).

Soon entire newspaper chains began declaring bankruptcy. In North America, the number would reach a dozen, including the Journal Register chain twice. The list included the owner of Canada's largest chain, media conglomerate Canwest Global Communications, which had taken on enormous debt in acquiring most of the country's major dailies at the millennium when an ill-fated 'convergence' craze saw newspapers partner with television networks. The owners of both Chicago dailies were in bankruptcy at one point. The giant Tribune chain had taken on a huge debt in buying up TV stations across the United States, and it became unable to meet the payments when the recession dropped its earnings. The owner of the tabloid *Sun-Times* was forced into bankruptcy after years of mismanagement by its former owner Conrad Black, who had also owned the *Telegraph*. Baron Black of Crossharbour, as he was known in the House of Lords, went to prison in Florida for five years starting in 2008 after being convicted of fraud at trial in Chicago.[1]

In the United Kingdom, cutbacks at newspapers across the country had already had a devastating effect by 2009. GMG, which owned local and regional newspapers in addition to its eponymous national daily, cut 150 jobs that March at its MEN Media subsidiary, which published the *Manchester Evening News* and 22 area weeklies. It made another 95 workers redundant from its newspapers in Surrey and Berkshire, reducing its regional flagship *Reading Evening Post* from daily to twice-weekly publication and closing its *Aldershot Mail* and *Esher News and Mail* (Burrell, 2009). The immediate cause of this carnage was a year-on-year drop in advertising for property (21 percent), cars (14 percent), and jobs (11 percent). The root cause, of course, was the Internet, which not only allowed anyone to be a publisher but also allowed anyone to sell ads. The classified advertising which newspapers once monopolised had already been eaten into by specialised publications carrying ads for homes, autos, and situations vacant, but introduction of the World Wide Web in 1993 had turned the market into a free-for-all. Marshall McLuhan (1964, p. 207) had foreseen the problem in his seminal book *Understanding Media.* 'The classified ads (and stock-market quotations) are the bedrock of the press. Should an alternative source of easy access to such diverse daily information be found, the press will fold'.

The consequences of newspaper closure were considerable. When the *Long Eaton Advertiser*, which had been published since 1882, was closed by owner Trinity Mirror in 2008, the Derbyshire home of 45,000 became 'a town without a voice', according to *Press Gazette.*

> The Advertiser is one of the rare cases of a paid-for title closing in a town where it had no direct competitors. Now this strong town has no paper, no dedicated radio station and it receives scant coverage from the regional press.
>
> (Christopher, 2010)

Long Eaton had 'almost ceased to exist', noted the *Guardian*, as it was getting 'lost in a more amorphous Nottingham-Derby conurbation' (Moss, 2009). When the weekly *Walsall Observer* closed in 2009 after 141 years of publication, the Staffordshire centre of 67,000 was similarly left without a locally produced newspaper. Two weeklies still circulated, but the *Walsall Advertiser* was produced 17 miles away in Tamworth, while the *Walsall Chronicle* was headquartered in Wolverhampton. As the *Independent* noted, 'Today, Walsall's nearest staff journalist is more than eight miles away in Cannock' (Burrell, 2012).

Scholarly research confirmed the social and political danger. After Trinity Mirror closed its *Port Talbot Guardian* in 2009, a study showed the South Wales town of 37,000 fell into 'a news black hole that has serious democratic consequences' (Howells, 2015, p. 281). The community, which in the 1970s had been served by five newspapers, was left with an information flow dominated by word of mouth, Rachel Howells (2015) found. A decline in coverage of council and other public meetings, she concluded, led to public confusion and lack of knowledge about local issues. 'The effects of this are in fostering rumour, speculation, confusion and lack of fore-knowledge, which seem to be linked to other effects such as powerlessness and frustration' (Howells, 2015, p. 282). Cutbacks at newspapers in Wales had long been a sore spot there. A 2007 Cardiff University study found that Trinity Mirror's subsidiary Media Wales published 42 percent of newspaper circulation in that country. Despite declining circulations, it generated profit margins that almost tripled from 13.9 percent in 2001 to 38.2 percent in 2005 by regularly increasing its cover prices, filling its pages with wire service stories, paying some of the lowest wages in the industry, and cutting 15 percent of its employees (Williams & Franklin, 2007).

Cardiff University lecturer Andy Williams found in 2010 that Trinity Mirror had slashed the number of editorial and production jobs at its Media Wales subsidiary by 41 percent over the previous ten years. He blamed the crisis in Welsh newspapers on 'mismanagement and greed by Trinity Mirror executives in London' (Williams, 2011, pp. 74–75). By 2015, Media Wales had cut more than 85 percent of its editorial and production staff, Williams (2017) found, from almost 700 in 1999 to only 100. Closures and redundancies brought by the recession reduced staff levels at some newspaper companies by almost half. According to one study, Trinity Mirror cut 47 percent of its staff between 2008 and 2013, Johnston Press slashed its by 46 percent, and Archant reduced its by 27 percent (Oliver & Ohlbaum, 2015). That was on top of a drop in local and regional press jobs from 13,020 in 2002 to 11,230 in 2007, a loss of 14 percent (Nel, 2010).

The political implications of newspaper closures and staff cutbacks were serious, studies had found. After the *Rocky Mountain News* folded and the *Seattle Post-Intelligencer* converted to online-only publication in 2009, civic engagement in Seattle and Denver was found to have dropped significantly (Shaker, 2014). A study by economists showed that the 2007 closure of the *Cincinnati Post* lowered the number of people voting in elections there and increased an incumbent's chances of staying in office (Schulhofer-Wohl & Garrido, 2009). A UK study quantified the effect of newspaper sales on voter turnout, finding that a 1 percentage point increase in daily circulation resulted in a 0.37 percentage point increase in local election turnout, while a 1 percentage point increase in weekly circulation brought a 0.1 percentage point increase in turnout. An additional daily or weekly local newspaper resulted in a 1.27 percentage point increase (Lavender et al., 2020). The cost of local government borrowing was found to rise significantly as a result of local newspaper closures because, due to a lack of press scrutiny, 'potential lenders have greater difficulty evaluating the quality of public projects and the government officials in charge of these projects' (Gao et al., 2020, p. 447).

The newspaper industry's pleas fell mostly on deaf ears when it came to the CMS committee, however. While it agreed that the merger regime needed to be re-examined and that the Office of Fair Trading should review the impact of local authority publications, newspapers were out of luck as far as financial assistance went. 'We conclude that in order to maintain the independence of local media it is not appropriate for the state to subsidise it' (House of Commons, 2010, p. 3). The committee agreed with Ofcom, which noted that the newspaper closures seen so far had to be considered in the context of a boom in free titles seen during the 1980s. Its analysis showed that of the 57 newspapers closed between January 2008 and February 2009, 49 had been weekly free sheets and that all of the remaining 8 paid titles were weeklies. The MPs made it clear that newspapers would have to find their own way out of whatever trouble they might be in, adding that they should 'innovate and re-evaluate the traditional model of local print media in order to survive in the new digital era' (House of Commons, 2010, p. 64). The committee noted that Murdoch had recently bruited the idea of charging readers for online access to content of the *Times* and *Sun*. 'If pay models were to be proved successful and widely adopted, this could change the economics of the provision of online news content' (House of Commons, 2010, p. 65).

Whatever strategy Murdoch adopted in response to the newspaper crisis would be influential given his record of bold success. No sooner had the Commons committee washed its hands of the newspaper industry's problems than he announced that the *Times* and *Sunday Times* would indeed erect paywalls around their websites. Murdoch became a paywall devotee after he bought the *Wall Street Journal* in 2007. His first instinct was to take the *Journal*'s paywall down in the traditional newspaper quest for the most readers possible to sell in turn to advertisers. Then he saw the numbers. The *Journal* was making more than US$65 million a year from online subscriptions, and because of the increased reader engagement paywalls brought it was also able to charge much more for its online ads than even the *New York Times*. Its online CPM, or cost per thousand customers reached, was US$55 in 1997, while the *Times* was getting only US$40, and search engines like Yahoo! and Excite were charging about US$20 (Kirsner, 1997).

The *Journal* was able to charge a premium, noted *BusinessWeek*, because its readers were considered more desirable by advertisers.

> The *Journal*'s readers are seen as business-minded, college-educated professionals with significantly above-average wealth – the sort of audience that advertisers, particularly makers of luxury goods, want to reach. If the Journal were to significantly expand its audience by moving to a free model, it would no longer be able to command the same premium because the audience would be more diverse.
>
> (Holahan, 2007)

The *Journal* began charging US$49 a year for access to its website in 1997, which dropped its traffic by more than 90 percent. Two years later, however, it had 250,000 online subscribers. It raised its subscription price to US$59 a year in 1999, but its renewal rate was 80 percent. In 2000, according to one study, the *Journal* recorded its largest ever gain in digital circulation, reaching 438,000 subscribers (Steinbock, 2000). But while paywalls worked for the *Journal* and its UK equivalent the *Financial Times* due to their focus on business, general-interest newspapers had proved unable to attract many digital subscribers. When the *New York Times* dropped its Times Select 'freemium' service and the *Economist* took down its paywall in 2007, pundits declared the experiment in paid content over (Ives & Klaassen, 2007; Palser, 2008).

But paywalls were far from dead. Its 'metered' paywall helped boost *Financial Times* profits by 13 percent in 2008, while other newspapers watched their revenues freefall with the recession (Hall, 2009). The *New York Times* spent a reported US$25 million to perfect the metered paywall it would introduce in 2011. Metrics had shown that about 85 percent of the newspaper's online audience read fewer than 20 articles a month, so the paywall was aimed at the 15 percent who were heavy users while allowing transient readers access for free (Grueskin et al., 2011).

Murdoch wasn't about to wait another year and spend millions of pounds erecting a metered paywall as the *New York Times* was doing. He ordered a 'hard' paywall erected around the *Times* websites in mid-2010, meaning readers would have to pay from the first article. The price would be £1, the same as for a hard copy, or £2 for weekly access. Print subscribers would get online access for free. International readers would be charged US$2 a day or US$4 per week. A monthly rate would be available for the *Times* smartphone app, which had proved popular since its introduction. One media buyer revealed to the *Financial Times* that News UK had also doubled its online advertising rates with the introduction of paywalls (Bintliff & Bradshaw, 2010). Murdoch also announced that *Times* and

Sunday Times articles would be blocked from Google searches, which led digital devotees to deride his paywall plan as misguided and him as a dinosaur. 'Rupert Murdoch has declared surrender', wrote American journalism professor Jeff Jarvis (2010, March 26) on the *Guardian* website. 'The future defeated him'.

> By building his paywall around Times Newspapers, he has said that he has no new ideas to build advertising. . . . Instead, Murdoch will milk his cash cow a pound at a time, leaving his children with a dry, dead beast, the remains of his once proud if not great newspaper empire.
>
> (Jarvis, 2010, March 26)

Like most Internet enthusiasts, Jarvis believed that online content should be free for all to read, interact with, and share. 'Charging for content reduces audience, which in turn reduces advertising revenue', he noted. 'And putting a wall around content keeps it out of the conversation and devalues brands' (Jarvis, 2009). Making articles available on Google searches was a net positive, he argued. 'When content is hidden, it cannot be found via search. In a link-and-search economy, content gains value only through these recommendations; an article without links has no readers and thus no value' (Jarvis, 2009). The City University of New York professor advocated letting Google link freely to newspaper content. 'Google shouldn't be paying newspapers – newspapers should be grateful Google doesn't charge them for the value it shares in links and audience. Google is their free newsstand' (Jarvis, 2010, January 18). In the weeks after News UK erected its paywall, Murdoch's move looked like a disaster as traffic to the *Times* and *Sunday Times* websites fell by two-thirds. By early 2011, however, unaudited figures showed that the *Times* and *Sunday Times* websites had a combined 79,000 monthly subscribers (Fenton, 2011). Murdoch's paywall strategy was working, at least at the *Times*.

Newspaper closures and cutbacks continued, however. One of the first dailies to fold after Enders made her prediction was the *London Paper*, which News UK had launched in 2006 as an evening freesheet published Monday to Friday. Given away at transit stations across London, it had been Murdoch's contribution to a glut of free titles that appeared across the world early in the millennium (see Chapter 4). Trinity Mirror made almost 120 workers redundant from its Midlands operations in November 2009, closing nine local titles including the *Burton Trader* and the *Coalville Echo*. It then reduced its 152-year-old *Birmingham Post* from daily to weekly publication while switching its evening *Birmingham Mail* to morning publication (Luft, 2009). The challenges facing local newspapers were illuminated in a study by Derby University lecturer Keith Perch of Trinity Mirror's *Leicester*

Mercury, which he edited from 2009 to 2011. Revenues at the paper fell by 60 percent with the recession and increased Internet use, Perch (2016) found, from £40 million in 2004 to only £16 million in 2011. The paper reduced its staff accordingly, from 508 in 2005 to 107 in 2011, a drop of 79 percent. Perch examined financial statements filed with Companies House by Northcliffe Newspapers, the Trinity Mirror subsidiary which published the *Mercury* until 2012. He found that its biggest drop in revenues came in recruitment advertising, which fell by 77 percent in four years, and property advertising, which fell by 63 percent in just two years during the recession. Some pointed to declining circulation as an indicator of newspaper health, but Perch found that copy sales comprised only about one-sixth of revenues at a typical local or regional newspaper. At the *Mercury*, circulation revenue fell from £5.7 million in 2007 to £4.3 million in 2011, but its drop in ad sales of almost half, from £22.5 million to £11.4 million, was what really hurt (Perch, 2016).

It wasn't just local and regional newspapers that were threatened. The *Guardian*, which had long been subsidised by its owning Scott Trust, had failed to make cost cuts commensurate with the drop in its ad revenues brought by the recession and the Internet, as most other newspapers had. Instead, it spent lavishly, paying £80 million in 2005 for new presses in London and Manchester to print its editions in a narrower Berliner format and moving in 2008 to new high-tech headquarters in King's Cross. Its sister Sunday paper *The Observer*, which was named 2006 Newspaper of the Year, lost £49.9 million that year. GMG, which qualified as a multimedia conglomerate with holdings in newspapers, magazines, websites, and radio, began to sell off assets. It sold 49.9 percent of its *Auto Trader* magazine to a private equity firm for £675 million in 2007. The recession doubled the losses of its Guardian News and Media division, which published its national newspapers, as together the *Guardian* and *Observer* would lose £100,000 a day between 2009 and 2012 (De Lisle, 2014). To offset the losses and safeguard the future of the *Guardian*, GMG sold its newspaper division MEN Media to Trinity Mirror in 2010, which included its flagship *Manchester Evening News*. It also made more than 300 staff redundant in 2010 and 2011, but it still recorded a loss of £33 million as revenues dropped by more than 10 percent. Its CEO warned staff that the group's reserves could run out in three to five years if radical changes were not made, including up to 175 more redundancies (Rayner, 2011).

The *Independent*, which was the last remaining national newspaper launched during a mid-1980s spate of start-ups brought by the advent of non-union printing and computer publishing technology, was barely hanging on. It was sold for £1 in 2010 to Russian oligarch Alexander Lebedev, who had paid the same price the year before for a controlling interest in the

Evening Standard. Lebedev then spun off a cheap, compact-sized version of the *Independent* simply titled *i* that was targeted at commuters and proved popular. Of the other quality nationals, only the *Telegraph* and the *Financial Times* were comfortably profitable, but for different reasons. The popular tabloids, which depended more on newsstand sales than on advertising and were less vulnerable to a recession as a result, continued to be profitable throughout the downturn, some very profitable (see Chapter 4).

But even after the economy slowly improved following one of the longest and deepest recessions in UK history, officially lasting a full five quarters from early 2008 to mid-2009, advertising never again graced newspapers in the quantity it once had. That made navigating their way out of the digital darkness essential for publishers. But in mid-2011, just as it appeared they might, the UK press was hit by yet a third existential threat, after the Internet and the recession. This one was of their own making, mostly Murdoch's. Competition for scoops and especially scandals had long been ruthless between London tabloids like the *Sun, Mirror, Express,* and *News of the World*, which led to little privacy for celebrities, sports stars, and even royals. Long-lens 'paparazzi' photographers pushed the limits of privacy law and often exceeded them, being roundly blamed for the 1997 car crash in Paris that killed Lady Diana Spencer. Reporters also often disregarded privacy concerns. What wasn't known until the phone-hacking scandal broke were both the lengths to which journalists would go in order to get information and their coziness with police and politicians. When that was revealed, calls came for the government to regulate the press despite more than 300 years of hard-won freedom.

The *Guardian* reported in mid-2011 that the *News of the World* had hacked the voicemail of Milly Dowler, a thirteen-year-old girl who had disappeared in 2002 (Davies & Hill, 2011). The revelation created such an uproar that advertisers began to pull out of the newspaper. The *Guardian* then reported that London police had found detailed evidence of more than 4,000 instances of phone hacking by the *News of the World*. Among the victims were families of soldiers killed in Iraq and Afghanistan and of victims of the 7/7 London terrorist attacks. Outrage grew as major figures in the Murdoch media empire were arrested. Eight would eventually be charged and five convicted, with three sentenced to prison for as long as eighteen months. News UK quickly announced that the *News of the World* would cease publishing. Its front-page apology admitted: 'Quite simply, we lost our way'.

The phone-hacking scandal was the biggest to ever visit the UK press. Labour leader Ed Miliband led calls for state regulation, labelling the self-regulatory Press Complaints Commission (PCC) a 'toothless poodle' and insisting that News UK be broken up for having 'too much power over

British life' (Helm et al., 2011). Former Prime Minister Gordon Brown accused News UK of 'law-breaking on an industrial scale', calling it a 'criminal media nexus' which had 'descended from the gutter to the sewer' (Wright & Grice, 2011). Summonsed by Parliament, Murdoch called it 'the most humble day of my life' as MPs ordered an inquiry into the culture, practices, and ethics of the press, to be chaired by former judge Lord Brian Leveson.

After sitting for thirteen months, the Leveson inquiry issued a four-volume report in late 2012 which ran to almost 2000 pages. It recommended replacing the PCC with a new regulatory body which would have the power to enforce a code of conduct, require the publication of prominent corrections and apologies, and even fine newspapers for violations. Instead, publishers created their own regulator, the Independent Press Standards Organisation, to which more than 1,400 titles signed up, including all national newspapers with the exception of the *Financial Times*, the *Guardian*, and the *Independent*. It was the first state-backed press regulation in Britain since licensing ended in 1695, but the UK press had at least avoided direct regulation.

Note

1. Black would be pardoned by US President Donald Trump in 2019 after writing a biography of Trump.

2   The Staying Power of the Press

Paul Linford circled 15 June 2014 on his calendar as the date by which Claire Enders predicted that half of the UK's local and regional newspapers would disappear. Linford had been a newspaper journalist for decades, working on local papers such as the *South Wales Echo, Derby Telegraph*, and *Mansfield Chad* before joining the regional daily *Newcastle Journal*, where he covered Parliament from 1995 until 2004 and rose to the position of assistant editor. He then went to work for Northcliffe Media, where he managed a series of digital publishing projects. In 2008, he started a digital publishing project of his own – a blog he called HoldtheFrontPage which focused on the local and regional newspaper industries in which he had worked. Most of what Linford posted was bad news. Circulation continued to drop, as did advertising revenue. The only thing that seemed to go up was the number of job cuts newspapers were having to make just to keep their heads above water. Some folded, but after five years Linford counted only 102 titles that had disappeared instead of the 650 Enders had predicted. About three-quarters of the lost titles had been free newspapers. The only paid regional daily to close was the *Liverpool Post*, which had been running a distant second to the market-leading *Liverpool Echo*. Trinity Mirror, which owned both, moved the *Post* to weekly publication in early 2012 before folding it in late 2013 after 158 years of publication.

Linford listed the casualties on his blog like a roll call of the war dead. His list actually went back six years to 2008, when 33 titles were lost. In 2009, the year Enders made her prediction, another 22 joined the list. After that the rate of attrition slowed, with only six casualties in 2010. Then it rose and fell again, with 18 listed for 2011, 12 for 2012, 4 for 2013, and 7 so far in 2014. The fluctuation could be explained, according to Linford, by the 'double-dip' economic decline of 2011–12, which followed a halting recovery in 2010. While not an official recession because it did not comprise two consecutive quarters of negative economic growth, the decline again dampened consumer spending with disposable incomes falling to levels not

DOI: 10.4324/9780429469206-3

seen since 1987. Again advertising fled newspapers, accelerating the rate of closures.

Despite what Enders told MPs in 2009, however, almost all newspapers continued to make money. Only a few nationals, such as the *Times* newspapers, the *Guardian*, and the *Observer*, made losses that had to be subsidised by their owners, and the *Times* and *Sunday Times* were already back in the black thanks to their paywall. They had more than 150,000 online subscribers by 2014 and recorded their first profit after many years of losses (Chittum, 2014). Perhaps there was life left in newspapers if they were protected by a paywall. Others eschewed online subscriptions, preferring instead to take advantage of the global scope provided by the Internet to attract more and more readers. Associated Newspapers, which was renamed DMG Media in 2013, continued to allow free access to its website MailOnline. It beefed up its digital staff in 2010, adding bureaus in Los Angeles and New York, and began to focus MailOnline heavily on celebrity news and other clickbait. Its digital revenues grew from £11 million in 2010 to £73 million in 2015 (Rigby, 2015). The *Guardian* also bet big on digital journalism, not only keeping its Guardian Online website free but also continuing to provide robust journalism while most other publishers were cutting back on their news staffs. The Scott Trust liquidated the rest of its assets in 2014 in an attempt to perpetuate *Guardian* journalism, selling its remaining half share in the *Auto Trader* for £619 million to bring its endowment above £850 million and declaring its newspapers 'secure for generations to come' (Press Gazette, 2014). The *Guardian* may have been losing tens of millions of pounds a year, but at that rate it could hold out for decades.

The *Telegraph* had long been the most profitable newspaper in Britain since a previous proprietor discovered the secret to making money in the newspaper business. Conrad Black broke a strike by *Telegraph* journalists in the late 1980s by publishing with only management personnel, which he claimed exposed 'one of the great myths of the industry: that journalists are essential to producing a newspaper' (Black, 1993, p. 405). In moving to new premises at Canary Wharf, the *Telegraph* left behind almost three-quarters of its staff and an annual loss of £8.9 million in 1986 turned into a profit of £41.5 million by 1989 (Siklos, 1996). Under new ownership since 2004 by brothers David and Frederick Barclay, the Telegraph Media Group scarcely noticed the recession of 2008–09, during which its profit margin stayed above 9 percent. Its profits grew to £61.2 million by 2013, made at a margin of 18.8 percent (O'Reilly & Edwards, 2014). The *Telegraph* introduced an iPad app in 2011 and in 2013 became the first general-interest newspaper in the United Kingdom to erect a metered paywall. Online readers were at first allowed free access to 20 articles a month but were then asked to subscribe for £1.99 a month or £20 per year (Greenslade, 2013). A 2014 study found that while the *Telegraph* had the UK's seventh most popular website, with traffic up tenfold since 2006, only 23 million of its 61 million unique yearly visitors were in the United Kingdom, concluding that the *Telegraph* 'had become a global proposition' (Schlesinger & Doyle, 2014, p. 12). In 2016, the *Telegraph* switched from the metered paywall to a 'freemium' system where access to its news coverage was free, but subscription to its opinion content was priced from £2 a week (Sweney, 2016, 3 November). Less than two years later, it changed its online course again, putting most of its political, business, and rugby coverage behind its paywall (Sweney, 2018, 3 October).

There was a dark side to the *Telegraph*'s business success, however. Its former chief political commentator denounced the newspaper in early 2015 after resigning over a 'collapse in standards' he claimed had seen it suppress coverage critical of advertisers, most notably of a tax evasion scheme involving the HSBC bank. 'The Telegraph's recent coverage of HSBC amounts to a form of fraud on its readers', wrote Peter Oborne (2015) on the website openDemocracy. 'It has been placing what it perceives to be the interests of a major international bank above its duty to bring the news to Telegraph readers'. Other examples of questionable *Telegraph* coverage listed by Oborne included a news feature on the Queen Mary II, which was owned by its major advertiser Cunard, and a commentary by the Chinese ambassador on pro-democracy protests in Hong Kong, on which the *Telegraph* had been oddly silent (Oborne, 2015). The *Telegraph* reportedly received £750,000 a year to publish a monthly China Watch supplement produced by state-owned newspaper *China Daily* (Hazlewood, 2016). A four-page fashion section, Oborne (2015) quipped, was 'granted more coverage than the Scottish referendum', while an accounting scandal at Tesco was covered only in the business section as the *Telegraph* focused on more positive news coverage of the supermarket chain. Oborne noted that the *Telegraph*'s foreign desk had been 'decimated' by cutbacks and that half of the paper's sub-editors had been sacked. A succession of editors had headed the *Telegraph* under the Barclays, he added, including three in 2014 alone. The latest was an American who instead of Editor was named Head of Content and brought what Oborne (2015) called a 'click culture' to the *Telegraph*.

> Circulation was falling fast when I joined the paper in September 2010, and I suspect this panicked the owners. Waves of sackings started, and the management made it plain that it believed the future of the British press to be digital. . . . Stories seemed no longer judged by their importance, accuracy or appeal to those who actually bought

the paper. The more important measure appeared to be the number of online visits.

(Oborne, 2015)

The *Telegraph* denied Oborne's claims of advertiser influence, but other news organisations confirmed them. *Press Gazette* quoted un-named but 'well-placed sources with inside knowledge', including one former staffer who said it had been the newspaper's 'dirty little secret for some time' (Turvill & Ponsford, 2015). So-called native advertising, which was disguised as editorial content, had become popular for its effectiveness, reportedly growing 40 percent a year (Southern, 2018). Many online publishers welcomed the revenue it brought, but most newspapers hesitated due to the long-standing ethic of separation between editorial and advertising content, which was known as the 'church-state wall', or in the United Kingdom as the 'Chinese wall'. Oborne (2015) deemed the adoption of native advertising by the *Telegraph* a 'sinister' development. 'It has long been axiomatic in quality British journalism that the advertising department and editorial should be kept rigorously apart. There is a great deal of evidence that, at the *Telegraph*, this distinction has collapsed' (Oborne, 2015). The *Telegraph* was sanctioned by the Advertising Standards Authority in 2015 for an article on Michelin tyres that was not obviously identified as marketing (Osborne Clarke, 2016).

The only real laggard among quality national newspapers, at least financially, was the *Independent*, which by 2014 had lost more than £50 million in the previous three years. Its only saving grace was its *i* spinoff, which was selling almost 300,000 copies a day at 20p. Lebedev doubled down on it, raising its price to 40p. Linford (2014) pointed out that, contrary to what Enders claimed, very few local and regional titles had actually been propped up by 'beneficent' publishers. 'Most were – and still remain – profitable.' He scolded Enders not so much because her prediction had been inaccurate, but because he claimed it had harmed newspapers.

The defining media narrative about the local press became one of irreversible decline. The problem with Ms Enders' pronouncements was that they were so widely believed at the time that they seemed likely to create a self-fulfilling prophecy about the future of the industry.

(Linford, 2014)

Press Gazette called the survival of UK regional dailies and their digital growth the 'great escape story of the media downturn' (Ponsford, 2015). It pointed to a turnaround at the MEN Media group which GMG sold in 2010 as evidence that Enders was wrong. 'She underestimated both the ruthlessness with which owners would cut costs and the determination and resilience of journalists themselves' (Ponsford, 2015). The *Economist* realised that it was wrong about newspapers being dead soon after the recession ended and retracted its obituary in 2010. 'Newspapers have escaped cataclysm by becoming leaner and more focused', it noted. 'The recession brought out an impressive and unexpected ability to adapt. If newspapers can keep that up in better times, they may be able to contemplate more than mere survival' (Anonymous, 2010).

Many pundits, however, continued to predict that it was only a matter of time for newspapers due to their declining copy sales. Greenslade (2014) came to Enders' defence. 'In strict terms, Linford is right and Enders was wrong. Newspapers, and the companies that own them, have proven to be resilient despite all the pressures'. According to Greenslade, however, newspapers would sooner or later be displaced by digital media. 'Enders's timing may have been wrong, and it's fun to tease her for being so specific, but her overall viewpoint is surely correct. Online is the future' (Greenslade, 2014).

The continued profitability of UK newspapers was outlined in detail by a 2015 report commissioned by the NMA, which had been created the year before by a merger of the Newspaper Society and the Newspaper Publishers Association. 'The UK continues to benefit from a remarkably successful news provider market', the report noted (Oliver & Ohlbaum, 2015, p. 16). The country still had the most national newspapers in the world per capita, it pointed out, and was second only to the United States in local newspapers. 'The number of titles published by the local and regional press has remained remarkably high and in contrast to the rate of decline in revenues' (Oliver & Ohlbaum, 2015, p. 40).

> Even arch sceptics of the durability of the print news business model in an online world are now recognising that predictions of the demise of the commercially funded print news media sector in the UK – and in other markets – have been premature.
>
> (Oliver & Ohlbaum, 2015, p. 30)

The report examined the performance of three of the largest regional press chains – Trinity Mirror, Johnston Press, and Archant – and found that the rate of decline in their print advertising revenue had slowed and that their digital advertising revenue had seen 'significant growth in some cases' (Oliver & Ohlbaum, p. 40). All three companies, it added, had seen their profit margin increase recently. Archant, which saw the largest decline in its operating profit margin, from 12.7 percent in 2008 to 4.8 percent in 2012, had recovered to 7.4 percent by 2013. 'In the case of Trinity Mirror, the operating profit margin has followed a broadly upwards trajectory for the whole period' (Oliver & Ohlbaum, 2015, p. 42). Despite its enviable profitability, however, Trinity Mirror continued to close local newspapers, shuttering seven in late 2014 with the loss of 50 jobs. The closures included all three of the publisher's Berkshire titles – the *Reading Post, GetReading*, and the *Wokingham & Bracknell Times* – along with its *Surrey Herald, Surrey Times, Woking Informer*, and *Harrow Observer*. An NUJ official called the closures 'sickening' and deemed them a watershed moment for the regional newspaper industry (Johnston, 2014).

While the profit margins of Johnston Press and Archant had indeed declined, in the case of Johnston Press it was from the 30-percent range prior to the recession. Even with rapidly falling revenues, its margin was still comfortably above 20 percent by 2014. The company nonetheless teetered on bankruptcy due to the huge debt it had taken on in making acquisitions when buying newspapers had seemed without risk. By 2006 it stood at £753 million. As a result, it had to squeeze out every possible pound of profit just to make its debt payments. *Press Gazette* called Johnston Press a 'zombie' company due to the debt which threatened to drag it into the grave (Ponsford, 2012, 26 April). 'The tragedy of Johnston Press is that, in the current climate, most businesses would do cartwheels at managing an operating profit margin of 17 per cent last year which it did' (Ponsford, 2012, 26 April). A former journalist for the *Scotsman*, which it bought in 2005 for £160 million, called Johnston Press 'the British newspaper company that ate itself' in the *British Journalism Review* (MacMillan, 2012, p. 65). 'Seven years later, the business has been sweated to stagnation. The website is a shadow of its former self. Resources have been slashed and hundreds of employees sacked' (MacMillan, 2012, p. 65). The only measure heading upward, quipped Arthur MacMillan (2012), was its cover price, which had been increased from £1 to £1.10 that fall, up 29 percent from the 85 pence it cost less than a year earlier. His harsh conclusion was that Johnston Press had 'wrecked *The Scotsman* and their own reputation' (MacMillan, 2012, p. 69).

A study of Johnston Press acquisitions in Ireland similarly pointed to concerns about the 'corporatisation of local news provision, the detachment of ownership from community and the sacrifice of journalistic resources to maintain operating profitability' (Cawley, 2017, p. 1164). Johnston Press paid £155 million to buy the five Irish titles of Score Press in 2005 and £95 million for the Leinster Leader Group of six dailies and weeklies to become the largest newspaper publisher in the Republic, but it sold them all in 2014 for only £7.2 million. 'The debt-funded sums JP paid to acquire the Irish titles created intense pressures to maintain very high levels of profitability', the study noted (Cawley, 2017, p. 1179). Facing bankruptcy, the company issued new shares in 2008 to pay down its debt by more than £200 million.

Its continued profitability allowed it to steadily pay off more debt, which stood at £302 million by 2013. Johnston Press also bought some time, persuading the company's lenders to defer payments on its remaining loans until 2015 (Boyle, 2013).

The MRC calculated in 2014 that 100 of the UK's 406 Local Government Areas had no daily newspaper, while 143 had only one. Media ownership, it added, had 'long been the "elephant in the room" when it comes to analysis of the state of our media: obvious to all but rarely discussed' (Media Reform Coalition, 2014, p. 1). The focus of the Leveson inquiry had been on newsgathering practices, it pointed out, and it had missed the larger problem of ownership influence (Media Reform Coalition, 2014). A 2016 study by scholars at King's College London confirmed the problem, finding that five publishers – Trinity Mirror, Johnston Press, Newsquest, Archant, and Tindle – accounted for 80 percent of local newspaper titles across the United Kingdom. It calculated that the number of local titles had declined by 35 percent in the previous thirty years and recommended a 'major upheaval of the existing media plurality framework' (Ramsay & Moore, 2016, p. 7).

Just as newspapers might have been celebrating survival past their predicted end date, however, they began to face an even more daunting existential challenge. The growth in digital advertising revenues which newspapers hoped would continue to help make up for their lost print advertising began to slow. Increasingly digital ads were going to Facebook, which had exploded in popularity to become the clear choice among social networks, and Google, which dominated the Internet. Few could have predicted at the millennium that the digital powerhouse to devour most of the advertising dollars which once went to newspapers would be an online search engine.

Most galling of all for newspapers was when this technology was applied to Google News, which hunted down articles for readers and listed them alongside the first sentence or so of their content. Newspapers were doing most of the work to report the news, and Google was profiting off it, according to publishers. The competition was killing newspapers, they complained, but the Office of Fair Trading saw nothing unfair about it. Its opinion to the 2009 CMS committee hearings on local and regional media was that Google had achieved its dominant status from successful innovation which had provided significant consumer benefits. The committee agreed, noting in its report that newspaper groups could opt out of Google searches but usually didn't because that would reduce traffic to their websites, on which their own advertising rates were based.

Johnston Press closed 11 free newspapers in late 2015, including the *Northampton Mercury*, which at age 295 claimed to be the oldest continuously published newspaper in the United Kingdom (Turvill, 2015). According to *Press Gazette*, that brought to more than 300 the total number of local newspapers closed in the previous decade. At least 60 had been closed since 2012, it calculated, including 23 so far in 2015. More than 100 new newspapers had launched in the previous decade, however, including four by Newsquest and five by Tindle (Turvill, 2015). As a publicly traded company, Johnston Press also had to worry about investor confidence. It collapsed in late 2015 after the company announced lower than expected revenues. Its share price fell by 11 percent in one day to its lowest ever, which continued a fall of more than 70 percent from the previous year and nearly 90 percent since early 2014 (Lewin & Mance, 2015). Johnston Press soon bought the *i* newspaper for £24.4 million, however, boosting its national circulation to more than 600,000 copies a day and making it the fourth largest newspaper publisher in the United Kingdom. It planned to expand distribution of the *i* into Northern Ireland and also began publishing it online. An NUJ official mocked the strategy as 'delusional', arguing that 'taking on extra debt and flogging off other assets will not result in salvation for Johnston Press' (Goodfellow, 2016). Going national made sense, however, since that sector was faring much better than local and regional publishing. While newspaper revenues overall fell by 12.2 percent between 2009 and 2013, one study showed, regional titles fared much worse than the nationals, declining 20.2 percent due to a drop in advertising revenue of 23.4 percent. National newspaper revenues declined 7.2 percent overall in that time, with advertising revenue falling only 2.4 percent (Research and Markets, 2014).

The growing dominance of Google and Facebook caused newspaper revenues to continue their fall. 'Even for an industry that has become accustomed to financial beatings, 2015 was brutal', noted the *Financial Times*. 'Print advertising in the UK fell by £112 million, according to estimates from Enders Analysis, equivalent to half Fleet Street's aggregate profits, or the combined wage bills of the *Times*, *Sunday Times* and the *Daily Telegraph*' (Mance, 2016). Spending on national newspaper advertising, it noted, had fallen by one-third since 2010 to £880 million. 'Now some in the industry are questioning whether there will ever be a profitable future . . . Profits at the market leaders – the *Daily Telegraph*, the *Sun* and *Daily Mail* – have fallen 40 per cent in the past decade' (Mance, 2016).

The sale of the *i* came as the *Independent* announced it would cease print publication and henceforth appear only online, making another 75 journalists redundant. Lebedev had lost an estimated £60 million on the national daily since buying it in 2010, as its circulation had fallen to only 56,000 from a peak of more than 400,000 (Armstrong, 2016). The *Independent*'s digital operations, however, were held separately from its print side in a company called Independent Digital News and Media Limited (IDNML).

It achieved profitability for the first time in 2014, moving from a £222,000 loss in 2013 to a profit of £449,000 after strong traffic growth (Sweney, 2014). Its 10 million unique users a month in 2010 had grown to 28 million in 2013, which was well behind the *Telegraph*'s 60 million, Guardian Online's 85 million, and MailOnline's 168 million (Sweney, 2014). IDNML turned a profit of £1.27 million in 2015, prompting the *Independent*'s move to online-only publication (Thurman & Fletcher, 2018). The news brought a renewed wave of predictions that all newspapers would eventually exit print. Journalism professor Brian Cathcart (2016) quipped in the *Guardian* that 'the paid-for newspaper is going the way of the dodo'.

> Sooner rather than later they will all go. No one can say in what order it will happen, but it will happen to the most venerable titles, even to the top-selling Sun and Mail. Trace the downward curves of print sales over the past couple of decades and then extend those lines into the future: you will find they all hit zero at some point in the next 25 years or so.
>
> (Cathcart, 2016)

The 2016 book *Last Words?* compiled the thoughts of dozens of industry analysts, academics, and executives, comprising a range of prognoses. Former *Guardian* editor Peter Preston (2016, p. 25) despaired for the future of print on paper. 'This is a moment for brutal honesty – the search for a successor business model to words on print pages . . . has wandered into a cul de sac'. Former *Sunday Mirror* editor Paul Connew (2016) predicted that the *Telegraph*, the *Express*, and the *Guardian* would all fail in the coming decade. Industry consultant Jim Chisolm (2016, p. 29) pointed to forecasts that newspaper advertising would hit zero in 2026. 'The problem is that the newspaper's reach of its target audience is no longer significant . . . . So a point is arising when, despite newspapers retaining some small circulation, their value to advertisers will be insignificant'. Chisolm (2016, p. 34) predicted that print would become a 'niche-only medium' within five years.

> If the current model of ownership and innovation continues, news as we know it will disappear from large sections of our society. . . . The current, profit-motivated business model has failed, and the shareholders of these businesses deserve what is coming.
>
> (Chisolm, 2016, pp. 34–35)

Other contributors were more optimistic, pointing out that most newspapers still made money. Former *Daily Mail* managing director Guy Zitter (2016) noted that it was making about £100 million a year in profit and the *Telegraph* almost £50 million. Archant CEO Jeff Henry (2016, p. 362) pointed to the continuing success of the *New European*, which his company had intended as only a short-lived 'pop up' weekly during the Brexit debate but continued to publish due to its popularity. 'Every single issue has been profitable. That in itself is an almost absurd achievement'. *Evening Standard* managing editor Doug Wills (2016) noted that after more than a decade of losses, the daily had recently turned to profit as a result of the decision to make it free, adding: 'There are now more newspapers read in London than ever before' (Wills, 2016, p. 145).

The newspaper business is a multi-layered enterprise little understood even by many who work in it and study it. To grasp whether newspapers will continue to publish requires an understanding of media economics and newspaper history, which the next chapters aspire to provide. Chapter 3 reviews the economic history of British newspapers, which aids in understanding how the industry developed the way it did. The bifurcated nature of newspaper publishing in the United Kingdom requires that the national market be examined separately from the market for local and regional newspapers due to their differing economics, so Chapter 4 looks at national newspapers, while Chapter 5 examines the provincial market. Each chapter benefits from an examination of newspaper company financial reports to see how their fortunes have fluctuated and to understand how publishers are dealing with calamitous change. Chapter 6 will attempt to collate this knowledge into a comprehensive understanding of the UK newspaper industry.

3 Press Freedom and Proliferation

The continental technology of printing that emerged in the 1450s was suppressed from the outset in England for its ability to spread powerful ideas, like freedom and democracy, which were dangerous to those in power, who then included mostly monarchs and religious leaders. They restricted ownership of the new devices capable of mass-producing texts, and they also controlled what words they could reproduce. The English Channel thus proved a veritable moat against the new technology for decades. The Tudors, noted Temple (2017), forbade printing presses outside of London except at the universities of Oxford and Cambridge. A royal licensing system was established, and prior censorship was instituted under Henry VIII in 1538 (O'Malley, 2014). The Thirty Years War, which began in 1618, increased the thirst for news, which soon filtered across the English Channel in print (Clarke, 2004). The earliest newspapers to appear in English under the Stuarts circa 1620 had to be printed in Holland (Stephens, 1997; Williams, 2010). The 1620s saw the regular appearance of bound newsbooks, which were typically 8 or 16 pages. The first real newspapers appeared as single-sheet corantos, so-called because they reprinted translations of current events from the continent, with interest then revolving around the Protestant Reformation and Germanic wars. Printed on wooden hand presses, which could easily be disassembled and moved, and sold by elusive street vendors of both sexes, the corantos engaged in a cat and mouse game with the authorities (Williams, 2010). An official complaint by the Spanish ambassador led Charles I to ban them in 1632, but the demand for news was so great that he granted royal licenses to two publishers in 1638 (Slauter, 2015).

The Civil War of the 1640s saw an explosion of newsbooks due to both momentous events and the weakening of royal power to prevent publication. Abolition of the Star Chamber in 1641 brought a 'breakdown of royal authority', noted Clarke (2004, p. 17) and thus 'shattered the chains of censorship'. Scriveners gathered facts and rumours from MPs and sold their published 'diurnals' unhindered from stalls at Westminster. Diurnalism, or

DOI: 10.4324/9780429469206-4

journalism, was born. More than 300 newsbooks were estimated to have been launched in the 1640s and 1650s, but most were short-lived. Of the 64 published by 1642, 30 lasted only one issue (Clarke, 2004). By 1649, 54 weekly titles were counted, each selling an estimated 250–500 copies per issue and up to 1,000 on occasion (Slauter, 2015). After the execution of Charles I in 1649, Parliament clamped down on publishers during the Commonwealth and the number of titles shrank dramatically. After the Restoration in 1660, Parliament passed the Licensing Act, which limited the number of publishers to a favoured few. The official government newspaper began life as the *Oxford Gazette* in 1665 due to the relocation of court there during the Plague, but it was renamed the *London Gazette* the following year and was estimated to have circulated between 12,000 and 15,000 copies per issue by century's end (Williams, 2010). It initially refused advertisements as 'not properly the business of a Paper of Intelligence', but it eventually did include paid notices (Slauter, 2015, p. 30). While financial accounts from the time are rare, surviving records show that the *Gazette* took in £1,135 from copy sales during the first eight months of 1707 and £790 from advertisements (Walker, 1973). The financial importance of ads was thus apparent from the outset.

Another upsurge in publications was prompted by the lifting of licensing and censorship in 1695 and fueled by a growing middle class, a thriving coffee house culture, and an emerging party system (Clarke, 2004). Many newspapers were distributed thrice weekly by mail, as evidenced by such titles as *Flying-Post*, *Post-Boy*, and *Post-Man* (Slauter, 2015). The latter two reportedly had circulations of between 3,000 and 4,000 copies per issue (Williams, 2010). The first regular daily newspaper, the *Daily Courant*, appeared in 1702 as a single sheet which sold for 1d and carried only foreign news translated from Dutch and French newspapers. Domestic news was soon added, but the *Daily Courant* struggled to survive with a circulation of only 800 and closed in 1735 (Temple, 2017). By 1709, according to Williams (2010), London had 18 newspapers, 16 of which were published thrice weekly.

The 1712 Stamp Act, which taxed publications by the page and also imposed a tax on advertisements, was aimed mostly at political pamphlets, but it applied to newspapers as well. It damaged newspapers economically, and according to Clarke (2004) led to fears of their early death. The effect was 'immediate and savage', noted Williams (2010, p. 62), as numerous papers folded or merged, including the popular *Spectator* and 24 provincial titles. The negative effect on growth of the press was only temporary, however. Larger pages were printed to get around the law, which resulted in the broadsheet newspaper (Williams, 2010, p. 62). Governments imposed taxes on newspapers not just to raise revenue, noted Slauter (2015, p. 29), but also to 'discourage the circulation of the cheapest newspapers (which they associated with more radical ideas)'.

An underground press of unstamped and irregular newspapers, which sold for a farthing (a quarter of a penny), flourished during the 1730s before being suppressed. The six to ten unstamped papers published in London during the 1730s and 1740s were estimated to have had a total weekly circulation of about 50,000 copies (Williams, 2010). To eliminate the unstamped titles, the government passed a law in 1743 which provided for fines and prison sentences for anyone caught selling them (Slauter, 2015). According to Temple (2017, p. 13), this brief flowering of a cheap underground press was 'an early indication of the prospect of a mass newspaper readership'.

Coffee houses flourished in the early 18th century, with 551 counted in London alone by 1739, and newspapers were a popular attraction, with as many as 40 patrons reading each copy subscribed to by the establishment (Clarke, 2004). Sales boomed accordingly, noted Clarke (2004), rising from 45,000 a week in 1710 to 210,000 in 1756. This contributed to a flourishing intellectual life during the so-called Age of Enlightenment, as citizens increasingly gathered to read and discuss the news. Habermas (1991) saw London's coffee house culture as a high point in communication history for the increased level of public participation it brought, but it was a privilege restricted almost exclusively to white, land-owning males. The brief flowering of a public sphere for the rational, informed discussion of political issues such as seen in London was soon displaced, Habermas (1991) noted, by a more commercial culture brought by advertising and other forms of mass persuasion. The culture clash became apparent early on, noted Barrès-Baker (2006), as the growing number of printed ads soon became a distraction for coffee house patrons.

> In 1728 there was a quarrel between coffee house owners and newspaper publishers. The coffee house owners wanted news for their customers to read, but claimed that up to 50 percent of material in the papers was advertising. The coffee house proprietors threatened to start publishing their own news, but nothing came of it.
>
> (Barrès-Baker, 2006, p. 21)

Ads were attracted by and mostly aimed at a wealthy readership. They covered a range of goods, from books, plays, wine, coffee and tea, wigs, medicines, cosmetics, lottery tickets, and servants, including slaves. 'These advertisements used visual gimmicks such as the ubiquitous pointing hands (which were still very popular in the 19th century), asterisks and wooden block engravings. They also made much use of "N.B." to emphasise features and benefits' (Barrès-Baker, 2006, p. 20). While the *Daily Courant* devoted half to two-thirds of its space to ads, other newspapers were as much as three-quarters advertising, including most of their front pages (Slauter, 2015). The demand for ads was so high that entire publications filled with them were distributed for free, such as the *Public Advertiser*, which first appeared in 1726, and the *Daily Advertiser*, which emerged four years later. The latter declared on its appearance that it would 'consist wholly of Advertisements, together with the Prices of Stocks, Course of Exchange, and Names and Descriptions of Persons becoming Bankrupt' (Barrès-Baker, 2006, p. 22). Surviving records show that the *Public Advertiser* took in £560 from copy sales in 1775 and £388 from ads (Walker, 1973). By 1783, according to Williams (2010, p. 68), there were five dailies in London devoted entirely to advertising. From only £1,023 in 1715, total advertising sales reached £54,890 by 1790 (Clarke, 2004).

By the 1720s, the official government *Gazette* was outstripped in influence by Opposition-backed papers like the *London Journal*. Robert Walpole, who became Britain's first prime minister in 1721, bought the *Journal* to defend his policies and had it sent postage-free to provincial readers (Slauter, 2015). Newspapers also supplemented their incomes with bribes from politicians, which one study notes were 'endemic' in the 18th century (Holmes et al., 2013, p. 7). Their precarious finances, according to Williams (1957, p. 31), meant that newspapers were 'almost always easily intimidated and still more easily bought'. According to Herd (1952, p. 64), Walpole 'systematically employed bribery to secure a favourable Press: during the last ten years of his administration [1732–1742] over £50,000 of public money was paid to newspapers and pamphleteers'. In the 1780s, noted Williams (2010, p. 66), Prime Minister William Pitt had two-thirds of London's morning newspapers in his pay, which was 'the key to his victory in the 1788 elections'. Theatre owners also paid 'suppression fees' to avoid negative reviews (Williams, 2010, p. 66). Articles known as 'puffs', so-called because they promoted a product or event, also became widespread. According to records of the *Daily Advertiser* from 1744, they were charged the same rate as ads but evaded paying tax because they were disguised as news (Walker, 1973). This was arguably the first 'advertorial' content or native advertising.

The stamp tax was raised in 1757 to finance the Seven Years' War, increasing the average price of a newspaper to 2½d, and again in 1776 to finance the American War, leading most papers to raise their price to 3d. The price increases did not deter sales, however. While in 1720 the London dailies sold about 800 copies each, the tri-weeklies 2,500, and the weeklies 3,500, by 1775 the dailies and tri-weeklies dominated with 2,000–5,000 in copy sales apiece. The first afternoon daily was the *Star* in 1788, which was also distributed outside of London by stagecoach (Williams, 2010). The annual sale of newspapers rose exponentially from an estimated 2.5 million in 1712–13 to 7.3 million in 1750 and 12.6 million in 1775 (Williams, 2010). The effect of taxes, according to Williams (1957, p. 29), was 'to keep the press on a leash, to tame it if it could no longer be suppressed'. High copy prices also conveniently served to restrict newspaper reading to the upper classes, he noted, reflecting 'the ruling class's fear of what might happen if newspaper reading were allowed to become general' (Williams, 1957, p. 29). In 1725, a newspaper typically cost 2d, according to Harris (1978), but by 1797 that had risen to 6d because of taxes and duties, putting it beyond the purse of most readers and suppressing the prospects of publishers. A press which had seemed 'on verge of honest achievements as 18th Century dawned', noted Williams (1957, p. 32), had been tamed by economic measures. 'Political independence ceased to have even the force of a distant aspiration. . . . They took their money and did what they were told' (Williams, 1957, p. 32). The effect was to keep the press under the thumb of government.

> Only if denied the hope of economic independence could the press be intimidated and bribed, changed from a potentially dangerous instrument of public opinion into the servant of government and factions: a tamed animal. Once tamed it became, as those bred for freedom often do in captivity, sour and mangy.
>
> (Williams, 1957, p. 30)

Books and medicines dominated advertising, noted Gardner (2016), as the London newspapers were then largely owned by booksellers and provincial newspapers were dependent on the book trade in London for advertising. In 1745, the *London Evening Post* carried an average of 29 book ads per issue (54 percent of the total) and the *General Evening Post* an average of 24 (75 percent). Lotteries to fund state building projects brought a windfall of advertising to newspapers starting in the second half of the 18th century until they were banned in 1826. In 1775, the *Annual Register* referred to 'lottery mania', and by the turn of the century they paid an average of £13,000 each for advertising, and as much as £20,000 (Gardner, 2016, p. 57). Newspapers were bought as much for their advertisements as for their news, especially ads for employment. 'Thus the *Morning Post* was the paper for gentlemen and gentlemen's gentlemen, ladies and ladies' maids; the *Daily News* for journalists; the *Daily Telegraph* for lower middle class employment and the *Daily Chronicle* and the *Echo* for the working class' (Holmes et al., 2013,

p. 8). Book trade agents were soon replaced by advertising agencies which were established, according to Gardner (2016, p. 165), 'in response to the sheer profits available in advertising sales'.

By the 19th century, newspaper profits were 'booming', according to Williams (2010, p. 81). A typical London daily which circulated about 3,000 copies in the 1770s took in about £23,000 a year in advertising revenues, according to Clarke (2004), and made a profit greater than £2,000. Ad sales at the *Public Advertiser* grew from £1,750 in 1766 to £23,612 in 1770, raising its profit from £950 to £2,223. The *Morning Chronicle* recorded £41,067 in advertising revenue by 1819, leaving it with a profit of £12,421 (Clarke, 2004).

Printers grew so numerous in London that many left it to set up shop in smaller towns. Newspapers began to appear outside of London as early as the 1690s (Williams, 2010). One of the first was the *Norwich Post*, which appeared in 1701 with articles reprinted from the London papers and no local content. Within five years it was making a weekly profit of 50 shillings and had two competitors (Clarke, 2004). The *Bristol Post Boy*, a two-page paper also consisting mostly of poached content, was probably founded in 1702 (Matthews, 2015). By 1725 there were 22 provincial papers, rising to 35 in 1760 and about 50 by 1780 (Williams, 2010). By 1790, there were 60 as the growth of provincial towns brought them into farther-flung centres (Gardner, 2016). Mortality rates for the press were daunting, however. Of the 150 papers founded in 60 cities across England from 1701 to 1760, half were thought to have lasted less than five years (Matthews, 2015). According to Williams (2010, p. 67), of 130 provincial titles which had started up by 1760, only 35 survived into the 19th century. By 1832, 150 titles were counted, and by 1851 more than 250 (Clarke, 2004).

Growing profits soon brought improved prospects for newspapers. By the end of the 18th century, two-thirds of provincial titles survived beyond five years, and they were often capable of producing several hundred pounds a year in profits. The *Chester Chronicle*, noted Gardner (2016), made profits of between £100 and £200 a year from 1783 to 1786, while the *Cumberland Pacquet* made more than £300 per annum from 1799 to 1805 and the *Chelmsford Chronicle* made £313 a year on average between 1777 and 1784.

> Yet many never made a profit at all, limping through a few years before collapsing in the face of low reader and advertiser numbers and established competition. Good business acumen was critical, for the chances of survival may have risen but so had the stakes.
>
> (Gardner, 2016, pp. 72–73)

As a result of their increased profits, the value of newspapers went up accordingly. The *Morning Post*, which had sold for £600 in 1795, grew so profitable from ads that it sold for £25,000 in 1803. The *Birmingham Gazette* and its associated printing business were sold for £4,000 in 1801 and a 50 percent interest in the newspaper sold for £4,000 six years later (Gardner, 2016). Provincial papers were flourishing by the 1830s. According to 1837–38 Newspaper Stamp Duty returns, noted Hobbs (2009), they sold about 50 percent more copies than the London papers did despite most being weeklies. The *Leeds Mercury* was the biggest seller in 1836 with an annual circulation of 270,000, while the *Lincoln, Rutland and Stamford Mercury* was close behind with a circulation of 260,000. 'At 7d these newspapers were expensive', noted Matthews (2017, p. 63), 'and individual copies were priced out of the reach of the working man – who additionally may not have been able to read'. The result was an extension to rural areas of London's coffee house culture, with newspapers gaining readerships of several times their circulation, added Matthews, with the most popular titles having around 30 readers per copy. Subscribers would also join forces to fund reading rooms, paying a guinea a week for a wide variety of reading material. 'In rural areas, landlords would buy newspapers for their pubs, and they would be read aloud so that content was made available to those who were illiterate' (Matthews, 2017, p. 63).

The high price of stamped publications drove some newspapers underground. A radical 'pauper press' emerged in the 1770s, noted Williams (2010), with these mostly unstamped papers advocating for individual liberties at first rather than class solidarity. The *Political Register*, which was founded in 1802 with a grant from Treasury to support the war against France, soon underwent a conversion, declaring that the greatest threat to Britain was not from abroad but instead from despotism at home (Williams, 2010). By railing against corruption, war profiteers, and bankers, the *Political Register* achieved a weekly circulation between 40,000 and 50,000 but folded in 1836 following the death of its founder. The *Poor Man's Guardian*, which was published for a penny from 1831 to 1835, sold between 12,000 and 16,000 copies per issue by distributing across the country from London (Williams, 2010). The authorities attempted to clamp down on unstamped newspapers in 1830, imprisoning 500 newsagents and one publisher, while 219 were prosecuted in 1835 (Clarke, 2004). The sheer number of unstamped titles made the law practically unenforceable, however, as they outsold official titles by a factor of ten. The *Weekly Herald* quipped in 1836 that 'a stamped paper now indeed is regarded as a curiosity in Bath, Birmingham, Manchester, Liverpool, Newcastle, Hull, Portsmouth etc' (Matthews, 2017, p. 67).

The heyday of radical newspapers was 1831–36, according to Williams (2010, p. 87), when an estimated 560 were founded. The Leeds-based *Northern Star*, which was started in 1837 with £690 raised by subscription, achieved a world-leading circulation of 80,000 in 1839 by promoting Chartism, or adoption of the People's Charter of 1838, which advocated voting rights for workers. It made a profit of £13,000 in 1839, according to Williams (2010) and £6,500 in 1840. It was published until 1858, by which time support for the radical press had waned with lifting of the Stamp Tax in 1855. The subsequent flourishing of newspapers saw their number increase more than eightfold by 1914, from 274 to 2,205 (Williams, 2010, p. 99).

Group ownership was common for London newspapers by the 1720s, noted Ferdinand (1997), with booksellers dominating the shareholders. Group ownership also became more common in towns outside London after the mid-18th century, according to Harris (1978), which in part explained a preponderance of ads for books. 'By the mid-eighteenth century group ownership was the norm rather than the exception for papers', noted Matthews (2017, p. 115).

> This pattern of complimentary interests was sustained into the Victorian era where newspapers were held alongside other interests, particular weekly titles, which though profitable, yielded lower returns. Of 216 newspapers listed in Charles Mitchell's Newspaper Press Directory in 1847, 115 of them had accompanying business interests, the most popular combination being the familiar 'Bookseller, Stationery and Patent Medicine Vendor'.
>
> (Matthews, 2017, p. 115)

Most provincial newspapers, however, remained part of a family business that also usually included printing. By the 1760s, according to Matthews (2015, p. 240), the most successful papers sold 3,000 to 4,000 copies a day but were 'expensive – the equivalent of £15 each in today's money – and would be exchanged and read communally'. In 1839, for example, the *Leeds Mercury* estimated that each of its copies was read by 15 to 20 people (Matthews, 2015). Just over a million London papers were distributed through the Post Office in 1764, its records show, but by the end of the century that had risen to 4.5 million (Harris, 1978). The freedom to cover parliamentary debates, which was not allowed until the 1770s, shifted the focus of newspapers from foreign affairs towards national politics and further reinforced their importance to public opinion (Harris, 1978).

John Walter founded the *Daily Universal Register* in 1785 with a loan from Treasury and found a market for it by selling copies for 2½d, while others sold for 3d. It was strong on financial news, market prices, and shipping news. It supported the government, for which it was paid a suppression fee of £300 annually. Walter then changed his newspaper's focus to hard news, however, and its name to the *Times* (Williams, 1957). It would soon revolutionise and dominate British journalism. In 1814, the *Times* developed the steam press, which was capable of printing 1,100 sheets an hour while hand printing could manage only about 250. This would aid its growing dominance, noted Williams (1957), as no other paper could print cheaply enough to compete. In 1817, Walter hired the first journalist to serve as editor of the *Times*, and Thomas Barnes boosted its foreign coverage and improved its management. According to Williams (2010, p. 84), Barnes sought to cover the issues of the day and 'deployed a team of shorthand reporters to cover meetings and events'. Further increasing its printing speed, as it did to 4,000 pages per hour in 1828, allowed the *Times* to increase its circulation (Clarke, 2004). It sold 3.3 million copies in 1830, which jumped to 4.3 million the following year, or seven times the sales of its closest competition, the *Morning Post*. Three of its eight pages would typically be devoted to ads, and it sold so many that it often had to print supplements to carry them all. Its issue of 3 July 1840 contained more than 600 advertisements (Williams, 2010, p. 106). The *Times* remarkably sold three times as many copies as all other London dailies combined for 40 years (Williams, 1957). When the 1832 Reform Act lowered the stamp tax on newspapers from 4d to 3d, the *Times* was printing editions of 12 or 16 pages daily plus advertising supplements three times a week, while others were only 8 pages. By 1842, its sales had doubled. By 1850, they doubled again, while sales of the *Morning Herald* fell by a third and those of the *Post* and the *Chronicle* fell by half (Williams, 1957). In the first six months of 1855, the *Times* sold 9 million copies while its closest competition, the *Daily Advertiser*, sold only 1 million (Williams, 2010). According to Hobbs (2013), a reduction drop in postal rates which attended the reduction in stamp tax by 1d in 1836 gave the *Times* an advantage over its rivals by providing cheaper distribution across the country. With a circulation of 60,000 by 1855, the *Times* could boast that its income was 'equal to that of the most flourishing of the German principalities' (Hobbs, 2013, p. 5).

London came to support dozens of competing newspapers, some of which survived through subsidies and political patronage. When the so-called taxes on knowledge were eliminated starting in the 1850s, the *Times* was well ahead of the pack and should have been perfectly positioned to outpace the new competition which spring up to challenge it. The duty on ads was abolished in 1853, with the stamp tax and paper duties following in 1855 and 1861 (O'Malley, 2014). As Williams (1957, p. 99) noted: 'It was as though a spell had been broken. . . . Almost overnight, new newspapers sprang into being in every part of the country, not at 4d but at 2d and very soon at 1d'. In 1855 alone, newspaper consumption rose by 300 percent, but it was mostly in the provinces, as London saw an increase of only 60 percent (Williams, 2010). The number of dailies rose by 78 between 1855 and 1870 (Williams, 2010).

The effect on journalism was profound, noted Williams (1957, p. 105). 'Never in history has there been so sudden and tremendous a flowering of the press'. Repeal of the Stamp Duty increased the number of provincial papers by 1871 from 289 to 851 (Matthews, 2017). More than simply helping them to proliferate, however, lifting the taxes also increased competition. Daily newspapers in 1855 were a 'desert' for news, according to Williams (1957, p. 101). Most provincial papers were small weeklies published by printers with stories copied from the London papers and a little local news, mostly from the courts. The spate of newspapers which sprang up within days of the stamp tax ending in 1855, however, tended to be 'strong daily organs of public opinion' (Williams, 1957, p. 105).

The abolition of the stamp tax actually brought the first golden age of the *Times* to an end by opening up the market to penny papers, especially outside London. While mail delivery had been free for all stamped newspapers, with repeal of the Stamp Act only those weighing less than four ounces could be sent without postage (Williams, 2010). Clarke (2004, p. 238) saw it as an 'act of revenge' by the government in retaliation for the *Times'* unvarnished reporting on the Crimean War. As Hobbs (2013, p. 5) noted: 'The official history of the paper is not alone in seeing repeal as a measure partly aimed at reducing the power of *The Times'*. It invested in new rotary press technology in 1858 which enabled printing speeds of 20,000 pages per hour, but it was in vain (Clarke, 2004). The bulk of its sales had been in the provinces, but the explosion in provincial dailies cut into its circulation there while the advantage it once enjoyed in foreign reporting disappeared with the telegraph (Clarke, 2004). Unable to cut its price below 3d to compete with the newcomers on price due to its high editorial costs and no longer enjoying cheap postal distribution, circulation of the *Times* was halved, falling from 71,000 in 1866 to 35,000 in 1903. After the 1880s, it was outsold by many provincial papers and became, noted Hobbs (2013, p. 5), 'less a "national" paper and more a metropolitan one'. The *Manchester Guardian* outsold the *Times* from 1890 until 1903, noted Hobbs (2009), and the *Glasgow Herald* outsold it from 1890 to 1907. Its profits continued to increase, however, because the *Times* still sold ample advertising due to its upscale readership, which was attracted by its focus on foreign affairs and business news. Having the 'right' readers, as opposed to the most readers, proved valuable in the emerging era of mass circulation. As Williams (2010, p. 148) noted, even small newspapers could turn a profit if their readers were 'deemed worthy of the attention of advertisers. Professionals with high disposable income helped a newspaper to draw in advertising revenue which more than compensated for small circulations'.

The abolition of newspaper taxes 'created a new environment for advertisers and publishers alike', noted Barrès-Baker (2006, p. 25), with one purveyor of pills spending more than £30,000 a year on advertising by 1855. The increasing dependence of newspapers on advertising starting in the mid-19th century, according to O'Malley (2014), favoured those which supported the status quo. Removal of the stamp tax allowed the use of rolled paper instead of stamped sheets, and making paper out of wood pulp instead of cloth rags lowered its cost (and quality). High-speed rotary presses using curved printing plates allowed two-sided printing and further increased output. The setting of type, which had been done by hand, was mechanised in 1872 with the giant Linotype machine, which set type in moulds cast from hot lead. In 1870, the Elementary School Act was passed requiring school attendance until age 12, raising literacy and creating what Williams (1957, p. 129) called 'the new public that was to change the face of journalism' because it was 'eager to educate and amuse itself'. The subsequent emergence in the late 1800s of a daily and Sunday press serving millions of readers, according to Wiener (2014, p. 206), was 'one of the significant events of the century'.

> It solidified the integration of newspapers into the cultural and social life of Britain and introduced many of the features of modern journalism with which we are familiar today. It transformed the publication of newspapers from a series of small-scale commercial undertakings into corporative financial structures that served the reading needs of a large portion of the population.
>
> (Wiener, 2014, p. 206)

By the 1860s, noted Wiener (2014, p. 208), 'a market for daily readers of newspapers representing a much wider social spectrum was in the process of being established'. Between 1870 and 1915, according to Silberstein-Loeb (2009), the number of dailies published in London ranged between 20 and 30. In the 1870s and 1880s, the circulation of morning penny papers ranged from 90,000 to 300,000. The *Daily Telegraph*, which began publishing for 2d in 1855 while the *Times* sold for 7d and others for 5d, emulated sensational US journalism and revolutionised British reporting. An unrestrained brand of journalism had developed in the United States due to a lack of government restrictions, and the result was a flourishing press which spread to every corner of the new republic but grew most rapidly in its growing urban centres. In cities like New York, a thriving Penny Press proved a phenomenon starting in the 1830s.

The *Telegraph* emulated the trend and started a price-cutting revolution in Britain when it reduced its price to a penny. From a circulation of 27,000, which was half that of the *Times*, its sales grew by 1860 to 142,000, which was more than that of the *Times* and all other London dailies combined. It eventually reached a world-leading circulation of 270,000 (Wiener, 2014). It also sold a new kind of advertising, which was classified by category of goods for sale, and it also developed the box number system for readers to respond to ads (Williams, 2010). Copies were increasingly sold not just by subscription but also on the street as corantos and unstamped titles had been. Under the so-called London Plan of distribution, which had been adopted by Penny Press papers in the United States, newsies bought discounted bundles on consignment and hawked them to passers-by. Evening newspapers soon sprang up containing fresh news aimed at commuters on their way home, attracting them with sensational, eye-catching headlines (Wiener, 2014).

Advances in printing eventually allowed the reproduction of pictures where before only engraved line drawings could be printed. Livelier writing increasingly emphasised human interest, sports, gossip, and sensational crime. Sunday newspapers first appeared in 1779, noted Williams (2010, p. 83), but their readership was low at first because 'the sale of everything but milk and mackerels on Sundays was against the law'. By 1812, however, at least 18 Sunday newspapers were sold in London, and by mid-century they were the most widely read newspapers. The *Sunday Times*, which then had no connection to the daily, proved popular in the 1830s by focusing on crime news (Williams, 2010). While less respectable than the dailies and more radical politically, titles like the *News of the World* and *Lloyd's Weekly News* grew in popularity in the 1840s, attracting a readership of workers with rising incomes who were eager for entertainment on their one day a week off (Wiener, 2014). As the press became more profitable through advertising, noted Williams (2010, p. 119), the focus of Sunday newspapers on radical politics was replaced by more of a concern for 'commercial gain'. *Lloyd's Weekly News* was initially the most popular Sunday title, selling 100,000 copies per issue by 1854 and a million by 1896 (Williams, 2010). The *Pall Mall Gazette* was founded in 1865 and shocked Victorian England with its focus on sex. Bookseller W. H. Smith refused to carry it, noted Williams (2010, p. 121), and 'many readers and advertisers were unhappy' with the language used and events described. This kind of 'new' journalism was influenced by American sensationalism, and it amassed large circulations for evening newspapers such as the *London Evening News*, which paid less attention to politics and foreign affairs in their quest for a mass audience. Between 1856 and 1881, total newspaper circulation rose by a 'staggering' 600 percent, according to Williams

(2010, p. 5). That was just the beginning, however, as an aggregating 'snippets' style of journalism attracted eyeballs with excerpts scalped from other publications in the absence of copyright restrictions, leading to a 'full-scale popular press' in the 1890s (Wiener, 2014, p. 210).

Alfred Harmsworth founded the *Star* in 1888 with big headlines, short stories, interviews, and bylines for reporters, soon selling 142,000 copies at ½d. He paid £23,000 in 1896 for the *Evening News*, which had never made a profit in its fourteen years. It made £25,000 in its first year under Harmsworth, more than recouping his investment, and it soon became the largest evening newspaper in the world. Its formula for success, noted Williams (2010, p. 127) included 'short paragraphs, snappy sentences and bold headlines'. But the *Daily Mail* which Harmsworth founded in 1896 at a cost of £500,000 (Williams, 2010) surpassed all others. It did so by becoming a 'true example of the yellow press', according to Williams (1957, p. 139). This genre of journalism went beyond sensationalism into the realm of fiction and showed the perils of unregulated, irresponsible journalism. It was pioneered in New York City during a *fin de siècle* newspaper war between publishers Joseph Pulitzer and William Randolph Hearst. It took its name from the Yellow Kid, the first colour comic strip character over which they also fought, but its wanton disregard for facts may have mistakenly set off the Spanish-American War in 1898 (Spencer, 2007).

After the *Daily Mail*, noted Williams (1957, p. 145), 'the world of journalism was never to be quite the same'. Despite London already having 28 dailies by then, according to Baistow (1970), its first issue sold almost 400,000 copies, or nearly as many as all the others combined. It attracted readers with decked headlines and photographs, sports and crime news, entertainment features, and a brief news digest to become, according to Williams (2010, p. 54), 'Britain's first truly mass circulation newspaper'. The brevity of *Daily Mail* stories was in sharp contrast, he noted, to the long-winded approach to news taken by its rivals, which were 'still happy to run articles of 6,000 words in length' (Williams, 2010, p. 129). It also eschewed politics, running reports of only a few lines on events in Parliament. The real secret to the *Daily Mail*'s success, however, was in selling eight-page editions for ½d, while most others charged 1d and the *Times* was sold for 3d. As Baistow (1970, p. 43) noted: 'The cheap national paper had arrived'. By 1897 the *Daily Mail* was selling 600,000 copies a day, and it soon hit 1 million during the Boer War. Its success in appealing to a popular audience with sensational journalism created a dichotomy between the serious press and the populars, noted Williams (1957), while its publication by a publicly traded company transformed the press into a major industry dependent on advertising. The *Daily Mail* began printing a northern edition in Manchester in 1900, which according to Hobbs (2009, p. 17) 'greatly improved its speed of distribution and arguably made it the first truly national daily newspaper'.

By the 20th century, the cost of launching a daily newspaper had increased exponentially, putting it beyond the means of most individuals, so limited liability stock companies became required to raise the needed capital. According to Williams (2010, p. 139), 4,000 newspaper companies were formed in the second half of the 19th century, and most of those formed from 1870 onwards were limited companies. This brought pressure from shareholders for dividend payments, according to Williams (2010, p. 140), so maximising advertising and circulation revenue became the 'driving force behind the newspaper'. While in 1855 a daily could be started for only about £20,000, by 1867 that had multiplied to £50,000, and by 1920 the cost of plant and machinery had risen so high that the capital required was about £750,000 (Curran, 2003). Advertising had so grown as a source of income for newspapers, however, that the potential profits were huge. Telegraph lines had connected European cities starting in the 1840s while undersea cables crossed the English Channel in the 1850s and the Atlantic and Indian Oceans in the 1860s. The telegraph transformed reporting, according to Williams (1957, p. 109), 'in some ways to alter it out of all recognition'. By the 1880s, telegraph news had become essential to daily journalism, with dispatches sent by wire to London newspapers from abroad by news agencies such as Reuters, the Press Association, and the Central News Association (Wiener, 2014).

The provincial press also grew dramatically starting in the 1850s due to the repeal of taxes, cheaper paper, and more abundant advertising. From 289 titles in 1854, their number grew to 851 by 1871 (Matthews, 2017). Not until the elimination of newspaper taxes was there a successful daily outside London, however, and only Manchester and Liverpool even had a bi-weekly newspaper (Williams, 1957). In 1855, the *Northern Daily Post* began publishing in Liverpool and the *Scotsman*, which had been founded in Edinburgh as a radical weekly in 1817, converted to daily publication. The *Glasgow Herald*, which first appeared in 1783 as the weekly *Glasgow Advertiser*, followed three years later.

The *Manchester Guardian* also converted from bi-weekly to daily publication in 1855. With a press capable of producing only 150 copies an hour, it had begun life as a radical weekly in 1821, selling four-page editions for 7d. With a new press printing 1,500 copies an hour, however, it grew by absorbing the rival *Manchester Volunteer* in 1836, and its circulation shot up to 3,400. It became a bi-weekly selling for 4d, and by 1842 it had a Saturday circulation of 8,000, the largest outside London, which grew by 1855 to 10,000 (Williams, 1957). The *Guardian*'s profits increased with its transformation into a mass circulation title funded mostly by advertising.

From average annual earnings of £6,777 between 1839 and 1844, according to Matthews (2017), the *Guardian's* profits rose to £12,000 in 1855 and to £20,000 between 1862 and 1865. The London papers, noted Hobbs (2013), could not provide the local news most readers across the country sought, as evidenced by their sales in the mid-19th century. In Manchester, for example, the London papers sold fewer than 2,000 copies a day in 1846, while the bi-weekly *Guardian* sold 9,000 (Hobbs, 2013).

By 1864, the number of dailies published outside London had risen to 51 and by 1889 to 155, while in the five years following repeal 120 papers were established in 102 towns which previously had none (Holmes et al., 2013). According to Clarke (2004, p. 125), the combination of railroads, telegraphs, rising literacy, and an end to the taxes on knowledge in the mid-19th century caused an explosion in publishing fueled by a 'flood of money coming into newspapers from the beneficiaries of industrialization'. The Isle of Wight, for example, had no newspapers in the 18th century, but by 1878 had ten despite a population of only 66,000. By 1900, a total of 1475 provincial titles were published, including 171 dailies (Clarke, 2004).

According to Hill (2016), the segmentation of national and provincial newspapers became more distinct with the development of an extensive national railway network in the 19th century, which enabled London newspapers to distribute quickly to provincial centres. Local dailies, which lacked the economies of scale enjoyed by the nationals, became more dependent on advertising for revenue and thus 'optimised the local content of their reporting' (Hill, 2016, p. 13). By 1864, there were 96 provincial dailies, compared to 18 in London, and their total annual sales were said to be 340 million, accounting for 62 percent of the national total. By the following year, 11 dailies were counted in Scotland and 12 in Ireland, while approximately 1,146 other newspapers were published throughout Britain (Silberstein-Loeb, 2009). By the late 1860s, most small provincial newspapers had circulations of less than 10,000, while provincial dailies ranged from 20,000 to 50,000. According to Silberstein-Loeb (2009), nationalisation of the telegraph in the late 1860s played a major role in the growth of provincial newspapers. Private ownership had led to cartels and high rates, but telegraph rates were kept low under public ownership expressly to allow for the social good of more widespread news.

> Telegraphy enabled provincial publishers to obtain their own news from London and have it on the street before the trains delivered the metropolitan newspapers to the provinces. . . . To make sure that all newspapers had equal access to telegraphy, the Post Office kept the price for press telegrams low.
>
> (Silberstein-Loeb, 2009, p. 765)

Equal access to telegraphic news, however, increased competition among provincial publications, according to Silberstein-Loeb (2009, p. 762), which in turn led to collusion and consolidation. 'The historical evidence suggests that free and open competition in the marketplace for ideas was a Utopian vision. Ubiquitous anticompetitive practices were the norm'. The provincial press thus began to contract while the London dailies enjoyed an increasing advantage in distribution. The balance between local and national newspapers had been 'fairly even' in the 1880s, noted Williams (2010, p. 117), but the extension of rail service tipped the balance in favour of the nationals. 'New "liner" trains were introduced in the 1890s to ensure that national papers could be transported to the regions overnight', noted Matthews (2017, p. 113), and these papers also began printing regional editions in cities such as Birmingham and Manchester. The *Daily Mail*, which had only been launched in 1896, was selling more than 700,000 copies a day by 1899, thanks in part to its ability to distribute across Britain by breakfast from a second printing plant in Manchester. The *Daily Mirror* similarly began regional distribution of a Birmingham edition in 1926, noted Matthews (2017), as did some major provincial titles. 'For these businesses, circulations and profits grew almost without faltering for the extended period of 1914–76' (Matthews, 2017, p. 113).

Legislative changes at the end of the 19th century further conspired against the provincial press, as local powers were reduced, making local politics less newsworthy (Williams, 2010, p. 136). The number of provincial dailies peaked at 172 in 1900, according to Matthews (2017), but fell to 121 by 1910 due to competition and amalgamation. The rapid increase in the number of dailies in the late 19th century was followed by a period of consolidation during which titles closed and amalgamated. In 1900, there were 70 provincial morning titles and 101 daily titles in England, but by 1914 this had dropped to 42 and 77, respectively (Matthews, 2017). Some became highly profitable as a result of consolidation and the disappearance of competition. The *Liverpool Daily Post*, for example, recorded annual earnings of more than £40,000 between 1900 and 1905 (Lee, 1976).

Concentration of ownership increased in both the national and provincial press sectors in the 20th century. By 1910, Harmsworth's company Amalgamated Press published 39 percent of London's morning newspaper circulation, noted Williams (2010, p. 140), along with 31 percent of its evening circulation. It also had 12 percent of Sunday circulation, 80 percent of which was published by four companies. Three companies owned more than two-thirds of morning newspapers in London and 80 percent of evening dailies (Williams, 2010, p. 140). Between 1921 and 1939, the percentage of provincial evening papers owned by London-based chains increased from 8 percent to 40 percent, noted Silberstein-Loeb (2009), while ownership of morning papers by chains rose from 12 percent to 44 percent. Rising costs established higher barriers to entry into the newspaper business, further discouraging competition. The cost of establishing a daily went up mostly due to the cost of new technology, according to Matthews (2015, p. 241), and increasingly it became a big business. 'In the 1850s it was estimated to cost £10,000-£20,000 to set up a London daily; 20 years later this was put at £100,000'. In 1881, she added, it cost an estimated £30,000 to establish a northern daily, with titles expected to generate around 50 percent of their income from advertising (Matthews, 2015).

Sunday newspaper circulations grew at an astonishing rate early in the 20th century, noted Temple (2017), with the *News of the World* selling more than four million copies by 1910. Daily circulations were still comparatively low, however, with even the market-leading *Daily Mail* selling only 900,000 copies. That would soon change, however, as national dailies still had another few levels to reach. Harmsworth launched the *Daily Mirror* in 1903 for 1d as a tabloid newspaper for women run by women, intending it to be 'a mirror of feminine life' (Finkelstein, 2020, p. 191). It was unsuccessful, however, so he re-launched it the following year with a male editor and a broader focus, cut its price to ½d, and ran mostly photographs on its front page. This was a successful formula, as the *Daily Mirror* was selling 300,000 copies a day within a year and 800,000 by 1913, when Harmsworth sold it to his brother Harold (Williams, 2010). According to Wiener (2014, p. 210), the success of the *Daily Mirror* as the world's first pictorial tabloid daily meant that 'the age of mass circulation journalism can be said to have truly arrived'.

Alfred Harmsworth entered the House of Lords in 1905, becoming Lord Northcliffe and thus the country's first press baron. His company Amalgamated Press was valued that year at £1.6 million, and he soon increased its holdings significantly. He saved the *Observer* Sunday newspaper by buying it in 1905, according to Williams (1957, p. 140). He urged its editor to avoid 'heavy politics' in order to increase its circulation, but his advice was ignored, so Northcliffe sold the paper in 1911 (Williams, 2010, p. 143). More importantly, noted Temple (2017), Northcliffe also rescued the *Times* by buying it in 1908. The *Times* was by then struggling with a circulation of only 38,000, but Northcliffe modernised its presses, producing a better-looking paper, and helped it to compete by cutting its cover price. By 1914, the *Times* was selling more than 250,000 copies a day, and according to Temple (2017, p. 16) 'had regained much of its old prestige'. By Harmsworth's death in 1922, it had a circulation of 318,000 (Williams, 1957). His brother Harold, who had by then been made Lord Rothermere, acquired his newspapers, except for the *Times*, for his company Associated Newspapers. The *Times* was sold to the Astor family, to whom Northcliffe had earlier sold the *Observer*. The increasing concentration of newspaper ownership in the hands of a few press lords aroused 'public disquiet', noted Williams (1957, p. 174). 'The age of big business in newspapers had begun'.

Magazine publisher Arthur Pearson launched the sensational *Daily Express* in 1900, which adopted the American practice of printing news on its front page instead of ads (Williams, 2010). It struggled financially for years, however, and to stay afloat it needed loans from the Conservative party, which it supported politically. It was losing £3,000 a day when it was bought in 1916 by Tory MP Max Aitken, who had first loaned it money in 1912 (Williams, 2010). A Canadian who would serve during World War I as Minister of Information and was thus in charge of propaganda, Aitken soon became Lord Beaverbrook. He invested in new presses for the *Daily Express* and hired top writers for it, turning the once dull newspaper into one that appealed to a conservative working-class readership with a crusading style, jingoistic news, and patriotic leaders. Beaverbrook perfected the formula of sensationalism which Northcliffe had pioneered, noted Baistow (1970), and the *Daily Express* grew into the largest newspaper in the world. From a circulation of less than 40,000 in 1919, its sales rose to more than four million by 1939, well ahead of the *Daily Mail*'s 1.5 million (Temple, 2017). It didn't turn a profit until 1922, however, by which time its circulation was 793,000 (Williams, 2010). In 1923, Beaverbrook bought the *Evening Standard*, which had been published since 1827 under a succession of owners.

Multi-column 'display' advertisements, often with illustrations, began to replace text-only classified ads starting in the 1880s, noted Williams (2010), and in 1896 the *Daily Mail* became the first newspaper to run full-page ads. By 1910, display advertising had surpassed classifieds as the dominant form of newspaper ads and then accounted for three-quarters of the advertising space of the *Daily Express* (Williams, 2010). The advent of department stores in the 1920s increased advertising exponentially, according to Williams (1957, p. 171), and 'opened up immense new fields of revenue'. This increased the importance of circulation and fueled competition during the inter-war years, along with consolidation. The result was the rise of a few large press owners including Beaverbrook, Pearson, Astor, and Rothermere. Independent newspaper owners were increasingly bought up by chains, noted Williams (1957, p. 178), often being forced out 'without mercy'.

There was also an increasing overlap between press ownership and the political elite by the early 20th century, noted O'Malley (2014, p. 231), as newspaper publishers were more frequently appointed to the House of Lords. 'By 1906 there were 49 journalists sitting as MPs, and the Commons and Lords between them boasted 15 newspaper proprietors'. As the cost of publishing newspapers rose after the 1850s, added O'Malley (2014, p. 230), a transfer of press control began from the working class to the business class which 'placed control of the press firmly in the hands of respectable and politically conformist people and organizations'. Proprietors like Rothermere and Pearson, noted Wiener (2014, p. 211), 'clearly were driven to capitalize journalism by the possibility of securing huge potential profits'. Newspapers were still published for their political influence, but the era of the Party Press was being eclipsed by the quest for a mass audience of all political persuasions in order to sell more ads. 'By the 1930s', noted Baistow (1970, p. 45), 'tycoons had taken over completely'.

Some newspapers were still subsidised by political parties and interest groups, however. The *Standard*, noted Temple (2017, p. 27), was subsidised by the Unionist Central Office, and in 'the most extraordinary example of political acquisition', Prime Minister David Lloyd George and Liberal Party supporters bought the *Daily Chronicle* in 1918. One socialist newspaper which unusually achieved a mass circulation was the *Daily Herald*, but its fate showed the increasing importance of advertising in an era of cut-price copy sales. The *Herald* was founded in 1911 as a strike newspaper and was re-launched the following year by a group of trade union activists as a daily. It proved popular with readers in a post-war period of rising socialist sentiment across Europe which was fueled by the 1917 Bolshevik revolution in Russia. By 1920, the *Herald* had daily sales of 330,000 (Williams, 1957), but despite its circulation success it could not attract much advertising and as a result lost money. 'Our success in circulation was our undoing', recalled its editor, George Lansbury, who was elected to Parliament in 1918 and would go on to lead the Labour Party in 1931. 'The more copies we sold, the more money we lost' (quoted in Curran, 1978, p. 70).

The *Herald* was taken over by the Trades Union Congress in 1922 and served as its official organ until it partnered with Odhams Press in 1929. Odhams heavily promoted the *Herald* with giveaways, discounts, and free insurance, offers which were soon matched by other newspapers. It also hired a small army of canvassers to sell subscriptions door to door. As a result, it was the first newspaper to surpass 2 million circulation in 1933, passing both the *Express* and the slumping *Daily Mail*. Still the *Herald* lost money. According to Murdock and Golding (1978, p. 131), its huge readership was 'unrepentantly working-class and hence unattractive to advertisers'. Beaverbrook saw the weakness in the *Herald*'s inflated circulation numbers and responded by improving the editorial content of his *Express*, which helped it re-take the lead with a circulation of 2.37 million by 1937 (Williams, 2010). By then the *Herald* was losing an estimated £5,000 a week, most of which it spent on canvassers to keep its circulation up (Williams, 1957). Beaverbrook's formula for editorial success was 'sophisticated escapism', according to Williams (1957, p. 234), with a romantic treatment of the news which soon saw sales of the *Sunday Express* reach 3.3 million. That was less than half the circulation of the *News of the World*, however, which focused mostly on crime news.

The circulation wars of the 1920s and 1930s saw a mushrooming of national newspaper readership, noted Murdock and Golding (1978), with total daily sales jumping from 3.1 million in 1918 to 10.6 million by 1939. By the end of the 1930s more than two-thirds of Britons regularly read a daily newspaper, noted Temple (2017), and almost everyone read a Sunday paper. The circulation of provincial dailies, which had exceeded that of London dailies by about a third in 1920, suffered as a result. The use of technology to achieve economies of scale with mass circulations reversed the pattern, and soon the nationals began to again outsell provincial newspapers. While there had been 171 provincial morning dailies at their peak in 1900, by 1921 there were only 41, and by 1937 only 28. The nationals were also able to undercut their provincial rivals, noted Baistow (1970), by using innovations such as the Linotype and fast presses to cut production costs in half in their battle for mass circulation and more ads to subsidise low cover prices. By 1970, the circulation of London dailies had almost doubled that of provincial dailies, which by then were mostly controlled by groups (Smith, 1970). At least 225 provincial weeklies folded between 1918 and 1957, noted Williams (1957, p. 4) as Britons 'read more and more copies of fewer and fewer newspapers'.

Increasing profits made the press a 'highly lucrative' business by the early 20th century, noted Williams, and encouraged its nationwide expansion by chains (2010, p. 138). 'Financial gain encouraged London newspaper owners to "dabble" in the provincial press' (Williams, 2010, p. 136). Chains of local weeklies had existed since the 18th century and chains of local dailies were established starting in the mid-19th century, noted Curran (2003), with Scottish-American multi-millionaire Andrew Carnegie owning a group of eight dailies and 10 weeklies by 1884. Reforms to business law in the latter half of the 19th century, added Matthews (2017, p. 115), 'extended the concept of limited liability to shareholders – and effectively enabled the limited company'. One newspaper that took advantage of the ability to more easily raise capital was the *Leeds Intelligencer*, whose owners formed the Yorkshire Conservative Newspaper Company in 1865 and a year later renamed their daily the *Yorkshire Post*. It issued 5,000 shares at £10 each to better promote the Conservative Party in competition with the Liberal *Leeds Mercury*.

Regional chains grew rapidly between 1890 and 1920, and according to Curran (2003, p. 10) engaged in 'spectacular consolidation' between the wars. 'For the provincial newspaper industry, the period of consolidation of ownership was most rapid between 1921 and 1929', noted Matthews (2017, p. 116). The five biggest chains went from owning 8 percent of evening newspapers in 1921 to 40 percent in 1939, and from 12 percent of morning newspapers to 44 percent (Curran, 2003). 'These groups would dominate the industry for fifty years', noted Matthews (2017, p. 116), 'and their influence persists today'.

Competition plummeted as the number of provincial newspapers fell as a result of closures and mergers. The number of towns with more than one evening newspaper fell from 24 in 1921 to only 10 in 1937, noted Curran (2003), while towns with more than one morning paper fell from 15 to only seven. As Temple noted (2017, p. 97): 'This is in stark contrast to the beginning of the twentieth century when, for example, Manchester had been served by 18 different papers and Liverpool by 11'. Ownership of provincial newspapers also became geographically concentrated, noted Matthews (2015, p. 243). 'Commercially motivated owners consolidated their positions by buying multiple titles to create monopolistic business models within defined circulation areas'. The industry thus came to be controlled by a few huge chains such as the Daily Mail and General Trust (DMGT), which was formed in 1932 by Lord Rothermere's company Associated Newspapers (Matthews, 2017). By 1947, noted Matthews (2015, p. 243), it dominated the Midlands, the Southwest, and Wales as one of four leading groups.

> Equally significant were Kemsley newspapers, Provincial newspapers, and the Westminster Press, formed through mergers and acquisitions among a close-knit group of associates. Between 1921 and 1946 these groups increased their total holding of titles from just under 15 per cent of total titles to nearly 43 per cent.

Westminster Press was created in 1921 when construction firm S. Pearson & Son acquired two groups of Liberal newspapers which together owned more than 20 morning and evening titles including the *Birmingham Gazette, Yorkshire Observer, Northern Echo,* and *Nottingham Journal*. In their early years, the groups had subsidised these party newspapers heavily. The *Northern Echo*, for example, received £66,000 in subsidies from 1904 to 1939, according to Matthews (2017), with most of that coming before 1918. After the inter-war industry consolidation, it became so profitable that it began paying dividends to its owners in 1935.

> Big profits meant that increasingly big players in this market sought to consolidate their holdings and reorganize their titles in a way which enabled them to make the most of their assets. The first thirty years of the century saw ... the growing domination of the provincial newspaper

market by a few, huge commercial enterprises in a relentless process which was interrupted only by the Second World War.

(Matthews, 2017, p. 111)

The corporate battle for dominance of provincial newspapers was Darwinian in the early decades of the 20th century, noted Matthews (2015, p. 243). 'Best equipped were those large companies who could resource costly circulation wars, often via the evening paper – a highly refined and profitable commercial product'. The result was a drop in the number of provincial dailies from 196 in 1900 to 169 in 1920 as competitors were closed. 'At the same time circulations – and profits – increased, making this a battle worth fighting' (Matthews, 2015, p. 243). After a long 'war' for provincial dominance, noted Curran (2003, p. 40), the Rothermere empire and the Kemsley chain, which was owned by the Welsh-born Berry brothers, signed a series of local treaties which divided up parts of the country between them. Kemsley, which had owned only four newspapers in 1921, grew to own 20 by 1939 and the brothers became Lords Camrose and Kemsley. Together with Beaverbrook and Rothermere, they owned half of the nation's press by 1937 (Curran, 2003).

4 The National Press
From Propaganda to Profit

One measure of the social and political importance accorded the British press is the number of public inquiries conducted into its health. No fewer than three royal commissions on the press were held in the thirty years following World War II alone. They were largely fruitless in reforming ownership of the industry, however, as publishers relied successfully on the libertarian ideal of press freedom to rebuff calls for regulation or even accountability (Boston, 1970; Boyce, et al. 1978; Curran, 2003; Harker et al., 2017; Jewell, 2013; Negrine, 1994; O'Malley, 2014; Ogbebor, 2020; Snoddy, 1992). The royal commissions did, however, chronicle a transformation of Britain's press from mostly a tool of propaganda to largely a means of profit (Curran, 2003; Hirsch & Gordon, 1975). Press resistance to reform, or at least effective self-regulation, eventually led to the phone-hacking scandal of 2011 and the resulting Leveson inquiry.

The first Royal Commission on the Press was convened in 1949 as a result of widespread fears that newspaper ownership was held too tightly by a few powerful press barons who used their power for propaganda purposes. Concentration of press ownership had grown so high during the 1930s that almost half the national newspapers were published by just three chains. The power over public perceptions this gave a few owners concerned many, especially since almost all British newspapers had supported the government's disastrous pre-war policy of Nazi appeasement. Many Britons began to question how well served they – and the nation – were by such tight control of the news. The NUJ, two of whose members sat as MPs, demanded an inquiry into the press soon after the war ended. Competition between newspapers was dwindling, it noted, as the number of daily and Sunday papers in Britain had fallen by almost a quarter, from 169 in 1921 to 128 by 1947. Public fears grew that control of the press had led to bias, political favouritism, and the suppression or distortion of news. Allegations were made that advertisers influenced content, journalists invaded privacy, and publishers kept blacklists of enemies whose names their newspapers never

DOI: 10.4324/9780429469206-5

mentioned (Snoddy, 1992). There was concern over diminishing local control of provincial newspapers, especially of those in the dominant Kemsley chain, whose leading articles were often written at company headquarters in London (see Chapter 5).

The first Royal Commission on the Press sat from 1947 to 1949 with a mandate 'to inquire into the control, management and ownership of the newspaper and periodical Press and the news agencies, including the financial structure and the monopolistic tendencies in control' (RCTP, 1949, p. iii). Its stated object was 'furthering the free expression of opinion' and its desired end was the 'greatest practicable accuracy in the presentation of news' (RCTP, 1949, p. iii). It heard from 182 witnesses, none more forthcoming than Lord Beaverbrook, who confirmed the worst fears of many when he testified of his *Daily Express*: 'I run the paper purely for the purpose of making propaganda, and with no other object' (RCTP, 1949, p. 25).

The commission's 363-page report found the British press healthy financially. About 4,000 newspapers were still published, it noted, including 112 dailies, local weeklies in 746 towns, and 9 national newspapers. Together they circulated 28 million copies a day to a population of 48 million. 'The analysis of the statistics supplied to us shows that there is nothing amounting to a financial monopoly in the Press and that there is at present no specific tendency in that direction' (RCTP, 1949, p. 81). The Royal Commission examined financial statements from most newspaper companies and found that their earnings doubled between 1937 and 1948, while their profit margins rose from 10.3 percent on average to 18.3 percent.[1] Only seven of 225 newspapers lost money in 1946 (3 percent), while 38 of 207 newspapers had done so in 1937 (18 percent).

> It was suggested that, in order to keep commercial motives within bounds, a limit should be set to the profits of newspaper undertakings. . . . Such a limitation would, it seems to us, be both unfair and undesirable, and would not achieve the purpose intended.
>
> (RCTP, 1949, p. 156)

While the number of national newspapers had dropped from 12 in 1921 to 9 in 1948, the Royal Commission found their number 'not alarmingly inadequate' yet 'not so large that any further decrease could be contemplated without anxiety' (RCTP, 1949, p. 176).

The nine national newspapers, it noted, were each separately owned, reflected the broad range of political opinion, and were 'about as many as a reader wanting a conspectus of opinion can conveniently study' (RCTP, 1949, p. 176). The Royal Commission found that any partisanship, where it existed, was that of proprietors. 'The policy of the Press is dictated neither by the advertisers, nor by the Government, nor by any outside financial interests. It is the policy of those who own and conduct the Press' (RCTP, 1949, p. 177). The Commission reported that it found no evidence of widespread blacklisting on personal or political grounds, and that the lists kept by Beaverbrook's *Daily Express* and *Evening Standard* were for fear of libel actions. 'Few of the names on the lists we saw were those of people of any importance and, insofar as the lists merely enjoin caution, they do not prevent the publication of news about a listed individual' (RCTP, 1949, p. 127). Fierce opposition by publishers to any suggestion of regulation as an infringement on press freedom led the Royal Commission to instead urge that the press reform itself.

> We do not see a solution to the problems we have indicated in major changes in the ownership and control of the industry. Free enterprise is a prerequisite of a free Press, and free enterprise in the case of newspapers of any considerable circulation will generally mean commercially profitable enterprise.
>
> (RCTP, 1949, p. 177)

Its main recommendations were for the improved education of journalists and the establishment of a 25-member General Council with one-fifth lay membership as a self-regulating body. It would, among other things, create a code of conduct; hear complaints; censure bad behaviour; and 'study developments in the Press which may tend towards greater concentration or monopoly' (RCTP, 1949, p. 174). Such a body was not set up until 1953, however, and then only after statutory regulation of the press was proposed in a private member's bill (Curran, 2003; Jewell, 2013).

Ownership concentration again increased rapidly starting in the mid-1950s. The post-war decade had enforced something of a holding pattern, after which the chains again grew larger and fewer. World War II had proved a 'godsend' for the industry, according to Greenslade (2003, p. 3), as sales and profits rose while competition, 'if not entirely suspended, was muted' as a result of newsprint rationing. This continued for more than a decade, causing a stand-still period for competition in the industry. When newsprint rationing ended in the mid-1950s, a shakeout saw several long-publishing dailies fold. The launch of private television network ITV in 1955 also brought increased competition for advertising, as by 1958 its ad revenues exceeded those of all national newspapers combined (Williams, 2010).

The advertising market boomed in the 1950s, but more importantly it changed fundamentally with the advent of target marketing. While ad sales had totalled £85 million in 1937, with £35 million (41 percent) going to the press, by 1954 they had grown to £280 million, with £160 million (57 percent) going to newspapers. Only two years later, the total had increased by a quarter to £350 million, with £210 million (66 percent) going to the press (Williams, 1957, p. 207). Circulations soared, with the popular press benefiting disproportionately over quality newspapers. The *Mirror* and the *Express* led the way, with daily circulation of the *Mirror* increasing from 1.3 million in 1937 to 4.7 million by 1954. In the 1950s, techniques of market research were imported from the United States which segmented audiences by demographic factors such as age, income, and education. As a result, noted Williams (2010, p. 174): 'Advertising agencies were also more discerning in their choice of newspapers as a result of the increasing amount of market research available to them'. This polarised ad spending between quality newspapers and the populars, noted Baistow (1970, p. 45), and left a 'gaping middle' without advertising support.

The closure or merger of several major newspapers in the early 1960s led to even higher ownership concentration. Despite selling more than 1.2 million copies a day, the *News Chronicle* morning national, which had supported the Liberal Party, was merged with the right-wing *Daily Mail* in 1960. Its owning Cadbury family received £1.925 million in an agreement which also saw their *Star* merged with the *Daily Mail*'s sister newspaper, the *Evening News*. The *News Chronicle* closure, the biggest in Britain to date, left 3,500 out of work and, according to Membery (2010, p. 68), caused 'tremendous anger among the staff that Cadbury had sold out to the *Mail* of all papers'. Three Sunday papers – the *Empire News*, the *Dispatch,* and the *Graphic* – were also closed by mid-1961. The London evening press 'almost vanished', noted Williams, dwindling to only two titles (2010, p. 177). By then two-thirds of national morning circulation was concentrated in three chains. The Mirror Group, which published the eponymous market leader and also took over the pro-Labour *Herald* in 1960, had 24 percent of sales. The *Daily Mail* was close behind with 23 percent, while Beaverbrook's *Express* had 20 percent, and he also owned the *Evening Standard*.

Amid fears that economic forces were spiralling out of control in the industry, a second Royal Commission on the Press was called in 1961 to inquire into 'the economic and financial factors affecting the production and sale of newspapers, magazines and other periodicals' (Royal Commission on the Press, 1962, p. 3). The terms of reference were 'extremely narrow', noted Harker et al. (2017, p. 254), and focused on 'structural factors leading to an increase in concentration of ownership'. The Commission counted 17 daily or Sunday papers which had disappeared across the country since 1948. While the top three groups published 67 percent of daily circulation, compared with 45 percent in 1948, control of the national Sunday market by the top three groups was even tighter, having risen from 61 percent to 84 percent.

Its report scolded the General Council for failing to follow the first Royal Commission's recommendations to name a lay chairperson, or even any lay members, and for neglecting to study and report on the factors leading to greater concentration or monopoly. 'Had they been carried out, much of our own inquiry might have been unnecessary' (Royal Commission on the Press, 1962, pp. 100–101). The Royal Commission obtained detailed financial information for 84 newspapers, including all of the largest daily and Sunday newspapers, and it calculated the profitability of quality nationals at 13.1 percent on average, but that of the populars at only 2.3 percent. A smaller gulf divided national Sunday newspapers, with the qualities making a margin of 12.3 percent on average and the populars 6.9 percent (Royal Commission on the Press, 1962, p. 186). Even higher profits were being made in the provinces, where evening and weekly newspapers were enjoying margins in the mid- to upper teens (see Chapter 5).

The Royal Commission rejected several suggestions for how to deal with the problem of growing ownership concentration, including breaking up the large groups; forcing the popular papers to charge higher prices; taxing advertising; limiting advertising, circulation, or chain ownership; co-operative printing; and government subsidies (Royal Commission on the Press, 1962). Instead, it recommended a Press Amalgamations Court to scrutinise the acquisition of any daily or Sunday newspaper which would give its new owner a weekly circulation of more than 3 million.

> The potential danger to the public interest of further concentration of ownership and control in the newspaper Press by amalgamations is beyond doubt. . . . The dangers can be eliminated at their source by placing some restriction on the power of newspaper undertakings to amalgamate or enlarge their newspaper properties.
>
> (Royal Commission on the Press, 1962, p. 103)

A telling piece of testimony to the second Royal Commission came from Roy Thomson, who like Beaverbrook was also a Canadian. 'My purpose is to run newspapers as a business', he said. 'To make money' (quoted in Negrine, 1999, p. 166). A one-time travelling salesman, Thomson had discovered how profitable newspapers were when he owned a radio station which shared a building with one in remote Northern Ontario. He soon bought it and then dozens more across Canada and the United States, applying a highly profitable formula of strict cost controls. Thomson Newspapers became notorious for penny-pinching, paying low salaries, issuing pencils individually, and requiring reporters to use scrap paper instead of providing them with notebooks (Braddon, 1968; Goldenberg, 1984). Thomson owned 19 newspapers in Canada by 1953, when he bought the *Scotsman*, moved to Edinburgh, and won the region's first commercial television license in 1957. He famously described Scottish Television on its opening as 'like having a licence to print your own money' (Crisell, 2003, p. 108). Thomson then bought the Kemsley group in 1959, which included the *Sunday Times*, establishing himself as a leading Fleet Street mogul at age 65. His next purchase, however, ran up against the scrutiny of press acquisitions which the second Royal Commission had urged.

Instead of a bespoke Press Amalgamations Court, however, increased oversight of newspaper acquisitions was delegated in 1965 to the Monopolies Commission. Thomson bought the *Times* in 1966 from the Astor family and applied to combine it with his *Sunday Times*, promising to preserve their separate identities, allow them editorial independence, and cover any losses they might incur. The Monopolies Commission called evidence which showed that earnings of the *Times* had fallen suddenly by more than half that year and that it had already discussed merger with the *Guardian*, the *Observer*, and the *Financial Times*. It heard from witnesses that the only hope for its survival was for a stronger organisation to take it over, but its report found that 'this belief may exaggerate the problem' (Monopolies Commission, 1966, p. 23). It noted in approving the sale that the purchase 'would not lead to an undue concentration of newspaper power' since Thomson would control only 6 percent of national and Sunday circulation as a result and did not own another national daily (Monopolies Commission, 1966, p. 24). Unfortunately for Thomson, noted Fred Hirsch and David Gordon (1975), the marketing techniques which had helped revive the *Sunday Times* did not work as well for the *Times*. Counter-intuitively, the circulation it added actually detracted from the demographic qualities which advertisers sought in the readership of a quality newspaper, which were primarily class and income.

> The *Times* slid downmarket on an expensive spiral. It went all out for circulation, and . . . it rose by a vast 69 percent to 432,000 four years later. The extra readers were bought expensively and they were not of the same social class as the existing readers.
>
> (Hirsch & Gordon, 1975, pp. 78–79)

Market research categorised readers alphabetically from A to E, with the A demographic comprising the upper middle class and B the middle class. A 'bizarre' advertising campaign designed to attract new readers, noted Hirsch and Gordon (1975, p. 79), emphasised that the *Times* 'was not exclusive, was not for Top People – was not the thing that made it such a good medium for display and classified advertising'. Adding extra readers in the lower-class C-E demographics, they pointed out, brought the percentage of ABs down to 43 percent (Hirsch & Gordon, 1975). This disastrous strategy was only reversed in 1971 under new management after *Times* losses grew to £1.4 million that year. 'By June 1974, the ABs were again 50 per cent of the readership, and in 1973 the loss . . . was a mere £187,000' (Hirsch & Gordon, 1975, p. 79). While the *Times* itself lost money, they added, its educational and literary supplements more than made up the shortfall, along with the *Sunday Times* and its magazine.

Hirsch, a professor at the University of Warwick, and Gordon, a journalist for the *Economist*, obtained financial reports for Times Newspapers and several other major newspaper companies, which they published in their 1975 book *Newspaper Money*. The reports showed that revenues of the *Times* rose 44 percent from £8.9 million in 1971 to £12.8 million in 1973, reducing its annual loss from £1.36 million to £187,000. Revenues of the *Sunday Times* rose 41 percent in the same period, from £10.2 million to £14.5 million, bringing it from a loss of £166,000 to a profit of £1.04 million. Adding the earnings of its literary and educational supplements, along with those of the *Sunday Times Magazine*, brought Times Newspapers from a loss of £87,000 in 1971 to a profit of £2.68 million by 1973.

Other national newspapers were doing even better. Revenues of the *Financial Times* almost tripled from £4.8 million in 1966 to £13.8 million in 1973, Hirsch and Gordon (1975) found, while its profits more than doubled from £1.05 million to £2.24 million. The *FT* had 'hit on the most successful formula', they noted: 'a low circulation (giving it particularly low newsprint costs), but a very select readership prized by advertisers' (Hirsch & Gordon, 1975, p. 74). While they were not able to obtain financial statements for the *Telegraph*, Hirsch and Gordon noted that it was reported in 1966 to be the most profitable Fleet Street daily since it sold about a third of all the classified ads in national newspapers. Classifieds were the fastest-growing revenue source for the nationals, they found, rising from £22 million in 1968 to £41 million in 1973. The *Telegraph*, which according to Hirsch and Gordon (1975, p. 80) had 'captured the hearts and minds of middle-class readers' and thus boasted more than twice the circulation of any other quality daily, was offered so many classifieds that it could not print them all.

Hirsch and Gordon concluded that the improved financial results of the 1960s and early 1970s reflected a shift in priorities by proprietors, as exemplified by the opposing aims of Beaverbrook and Thomson. While both propaganda and profit had been the prerogative of early press barons, they noted, a sea change had taken place towards the latter. 'The press lords of the present generation have shown a general change of emphasis and style. These tycoons in business accountancy are less interested in what their newspapers say than in what they pay' (Hirsch & Gordon, 1975, p. 39).

Since its fiscal year ended on 31 March, they were able to get figures from early 1974 for IPC Newspapers, which had acquired the *Mirror* in 1963, and they showed an ominous trend. *Mirror* profits fell sharply in its 1973–74 fiscal year, when a recession began. *Sunday People*, which IPC also published, suffered even worse, falling to a loss of £944,000 that year (Hirsch & Gordon, 1975). The recession, which began in mid-1973 and deepened with the OPEC oil embargo that fall, saw GDP fall by 2.7 percent in Britain during the first quarter of 1974 alone. A second 'double-dip' recession soon followed in mid-1975 and was unusually characterised by simultaneous inflation and high unemployment, or 'stagflation', which caused the United Kingdom to become known as the 'sick man' of Europe. Rising prices brought industrial unrest, and the strikes and lockouts increased in frequency and ferocity into the mid-1980s.

These economic problems exposed the financial weakness in Britain's newspaper industry, which had been alluded to by the 1961–62 Royal Commission as the problem of 'efficiency'. High labour costs had resulted from publishers acceding easily to union demands in order to avoid publication interruptions which could prove disastrous in such a highly competitive market. The wages of manual workers in the newspaper industry were the highest of any in the country, it noted, a problem exacerbated by manning clauses in union contracts which often required many more union members to be employed than were necessary, especially under rising levels of automation. The 1961–62 Royal Commission had asked Mirror Newspapers to examine its staffing for possible savings, and it found that nearly 40 percent of its wage earners could have been dispensed with.

> The trades unions for their part – some more than others – have taken continuing prosperity for granted in pressing for high earnings and high manning standards regardless of the level of productivity. . . . Some are now beginning to realize that inefficiency may help to kill at least some of the geese which lay the reputedly golden eggs.
>
> (Royal Commission on the Press, 1962, p. 32)

The combination of a falling economy and high labour costs was made worse for newspapers by rising newsprint prices, which doubled between 1972 and 1974. They could not raise their cover prices, however, because they were controlled under government anti-inflation measures. Newspapers thus became caught in a squeeze between rising costs and falling revenues, which soon resulted in more closures. The *Daily Sketch* merged in 1971 with the *Daily Mail*. The *Scottish Daily Express* folded in 1974, putting 1,800 out of work. By the end of 1974, half of Fleet Street was making a loss and its newspapers had to be subsidised by sister publications or their owners' other business interests, noted Hirsch and Gordon (1975, pp. 116–117). 'If each newspaper had to stand or fall on its own commercial merits, four of the eight national dailies in late 1974 would cease publication'.

As a result, a third Royal Commission on the Press was called in 1974 to help sort its labour problems. While its terms of reference also included investigating the ineffective Press Council, noted Harker et al. (2017, p. 259), it was 'dominated by questions concerning the economics of newspaper production, management and labour relations, and market concentration'. Meanwhile, conditions in the industry had so deteriorated that publishers approached the Commission in 1975 and suggested an interim report into what they described as 'a crisis of unprecedented dimensions and dangers' (RCTP, 1977a, p. 3). It was issued in 1976 and noted that '1974 and 1975 were two consecutive bad years for the industry, though the populars improved their profits significantly in 1975. Only three dailies and three Sundays made profits, and in 1975 only four dailies and one Sunday did so' (RCTP, 1976, pp. 4–5).

Circulation fell sharply in 1975, the interim report noted, with Sunday popular newspapers hardest hit. 'The fall in circulation for most titles between 1974 and 1975 was the sharpest for many years' (RCTP, 1976, p. 38). A similar sharp decline in advertising revenue affected the quality dailies most because they derived 58 percent of their revenue from that source, compared with only 27 percent for the populars, which relied more on circulation sales. Ad revenue declined by nearly £6 million or 3.5 percent between 1974 and 1975 led by classifieds, which fell by 19 percent. Quality morning newspapers as a result made steep losses in 1975. 'They suffered an adverse cash flow of over £10 million on a turnover of £116 millions. . . . the condition of the two London evening papers is more serious still' (RCTP, 1976, p. 5). Popular papers bounced back in 1975 after incurring only minor losses in 1973–74, but the losses of quality dailies more than doubled from £1.6 million to £3.8 million in 1975 and for quality Sundays from £1.1 million to £3 million. 'The mere continuation of losses and of the even more adverse cash flow, has a cumulative effect which in some cases is becoming critical' (RCTP, 1976, p. 6). The earnings of production employees in Fleet Street, the interim report noted, were 60–70 percent higher than the national average for male manual labour by 1975, leaving newspapers squeezed even more between high costs and falling revenues. 'The only means of improving their prospects of survival is substantial savings in cost, as quickly as possible' (RCTP, 1976, p. 7).

The subtext to the problem of high labour costs on Fleet Street was new technology already in use at some non-union provincial papers. It provided enormous cost savings by eliminating entire classes of workers, but it required considerable capital outlay for computerisation, which the quality newspapers in particular could not afford. 'The cost of the new technology ranges from £2-£3 million per house', noted the Royal Commission's interim report, 'with an estimated total of some £20 million over a period of up to four years for the national newspaper industry as a whole' (RCTP, 1976, p. 7). Computerisation would reduce labour costs by 25 percent and make redundant the printers who had once set type by hand and then out of molten lead. Photographic typesetting, which instead set type on strips of paper printed from a computer terminal, was already standard at many smaller newspapers, and full computerisation was in place at some provincial publishers. It eliminated the need for typesetting entirely, as once a reporter typed a story into the computer's memory, it did not need to be re-keyed.

The Royal Commission asked the Advisory, Conciliation and Arbitration Service to investigate industrial relations in the national newspaper industry, and it published a report at the end of 1976. In it, union leadership agreed a plan with publishers to introduce the new technology in conjunction with voluntary redundancy and pensions, but it was rejected in early 1977 by the memberships of all Fleet Street unions except the NUJ. By the time the Royal Commission's final report was released in mid-1977, industrial action had taken a toll on Fleet Street. The report estimated that between October 1976 and March 1977 about 45 million copies of daily and Sunday newspapers had been lost due to production interruptions, a 50 percent increase from a year earlier (Royal Commission on the Press, 1977). *The Times* failed to appear for six consecutive days as a result of industrial action in early 1977. 'Events such as these would have been unthinkable until a few years ago; now they are commonplace', noted the Royal Commission report. 'If this suicidal behaviour persists, it is a safe prediction that Fleet Street will experience the fate of New York where five newspapers were killed in the decade before 1975' (Royal Commission on the Press, 1977, p. 226).

The report noted that while ownership concentration had increased since 1961, with the number of UK publishers falling to 220 from more than 490, it had not reached a level 'where the public interest has been damaged' (Royal Commission on the Press, 1977, p. 134). As a result of takeovers, however, ownership had increased by large conglomerates which also owned other businesses. Most notable were book publisher Pearson, which acquired the *Financial Times* in 1957, oil company Atlantic Richfield, which bought the *Observer* in 1976, and paper maker Reed International, which merged in 1970 with IPC, the owner of Daily Mirror Newspapers. The *Daily Telegraph* continued to lead in sales of quality nationals, with 56 percent of the market, while Thomson's share had increased from 7 percent in 1961 to 20 percent in 1976 with his purchase of the *Times*. The Royal Commission again declined to take serious action against ownership concentration but warned against its growth. 'For reasons that relate more to preserving editorial variety than to economics, we take the view that, in the United Kingdom as a whole, concentration of ownership should not be permitted to grow inexorably' (Royal Commission on the Press, 1977, p. 134).

The Royal Commission report ruled out setting a maximum size for publishers, subsidising new entrants to the market, or requiring divestiture to reduce concentration. It instead recommended tightening the rules to subject newspaper acquisitions by existing proprietors to 'sharp public scrutiny' (Royal Commission on the Press, 1977, p. 138). It urged lowering from 500,000 to 200,000 the level of daily circulation above which companies had to obtain consent for acquisitions, and reconsidering the practice of not referring to the Monopolies Commission the transfer of newspapers under 25,000 in circulation. It also urged that the public interest be considered for the first time in newspaper ownership changes. 'Consent to newspaper mergers both national and provincial should be withheld unless the Monopolies and Mergers Commission report that they are satisfied that the merger will not operate against the public interest' (Royal Commission on the Press, 1977, p. 231).

The national newspaper industry, however, became increasingly dominated in the 1970s by one man who transformed it first with a new type of journalism, and then in the 1980s with a new industrial relations paradigm brought by imposing the long-awaited new technology. Murdoch's makeover helped the *Sun* overtake the *Daily Mirror* as the UK's largest-circulation daily in 1978 and he soon stopped its support for Labour, backing Conservative candidate Margaret Thatcher for prime minister in the 1979 election. Her victory began a lucrative partnership, according to Simpson (2010, p. 486), as in return for Murdoch's support, 'Thatcher was able to reward him in ways that . . . would bring him large amounts of money' (Simpson, 2010).

> It was always clear that his papers would support whatever line Murdoch thought would help his group's profits. . . . And the price Mrs Thatcher was willing to pay in return for this service was her agreement to allow Murdoch's business interests to thrive, without too much interference from the watchdogs whose job it was to protect the public against the concentration of control in the hands of media barons.
>
> (Simpson, 2010, pp. 486–487)

An attempt by Thomson to introduce new technology at Times Newspapers in the late 1970s led to fierce resistance from its unions. Roy Thomson died in 1976 and left leadership of the chain he founded to his son Ken, who decided to shut down the *Times* and *Sunday Times* in late 1978 until an agreement could be reached on computerisation. None was achieved, prompting Thomson to keep the newspapers off their presses for eleven months. On finally resuming publication, the younger Thomson resolved to sell Times Newspapers and focus instead on more profitable US acquisitions (Goldenberg, 1984). Murdoch bought the historic titles, which gave him leading quality and popular dailies, plus two Sunday newspapers. It also brought ownership concentration to a new high. The purchase should have been referred to the Monopolies Commission, but Thatcher allowed Murdoch to do an end run around the requirement in early 1981 by having Times Newspapers declared a failing business. Former *Sunday Times* editor Sir Harold Evans (2015) claimed that financial results for the newspaper were altered to make it appear that Times Newspapers was losing money. Evans, who was elevated to editor of the *Times* by Murdoch before being forced out in 1982, called it 'the coup that transformed the relationship between British politics and journalism'. Murdoch also promised to maintain the editorial independence of the *Times* and *Sunday Times* but, according to Evans (2015), 'broke every one of those promises in the first years'.

Murdoch was able to persuade the unions to allow photocomposition at Times Newspapers, which reduced the number of printers by half, but not full computerisation. Thatcher's assistance proved vital to Murdoch in then moving his newspapers to non-union facilities at Wapping in 1986 by providing an overwhelming police presence against mass union picketing. It continued for more than a year in what Temple (2008, p. 77) called 'one of the bitterest industrial disputes in British trade union history'. Murdoch's success in breaking the unions began an exodus by publishers from Fleet Street to new printing plants which did not need such an expensive labour force. The move to non-union production reduced Murdoch's annual costs by almost £80 million (Williams, 2010). As a result, profits for the *Sun* and *News of the World* rose from £16 million in 1986 to £124 million in 1988, with a profit margin of 42 percent (Lewis et al., 2008). As Snoddy (1992, p. 14) noted: 'In a remarkable period of little more than two months at the beginning of 1986, the national newspaper industry was transformed'.

The final transformation of the UK national press resulted not from any technological advancement but rather from *fin de siècle* innovation. Inspired by the worldwide success of Swedish firm Metro International, DMGT pioneered free commuter tabloids in 1999, launching its *Metro* in London with an initial press run of 85,000. It soon expanded the no-frills, apolitical daily to other major cities, including Manchester and Birmingham. It spread in 2004 to Nottingham, Bristol, and Bath, then in 2005 to Dublin. DMGT also entered into a joint venture with Trinity Mirror in 2006 to publish *Metro* editions in Cardiff and Liverpool. The Metro chain eventually included more than a dozen regional editions across the British Isles, some also produced jointly with Johnston Press.

By 2005, the London *Metro* was giving away a half million copies every Monday through Friday, which Murdoch estimated stole between 30,000 and 40,000 readers a day from his *Sun* (Tryhorn, 2005). Its success prompted a spate of competitors. In 2004, the *Evening Standard* began free distribution of a stripped-down mid-afternoon version called *Standard Lite*. *City A.M.* was launched in 2005, and the following year News UK launched an evening freesheet called the *London Paper*. DMGT launched *Evening Lite* as a 'spoiler' to protect against the p.m. competition. Even the *Financial Times* got into the act, launching *FTpm* (Franklin, 2006). The 2008–09 recession, however, dried up most of the advertising revenue on which every free newspaper depends, and *Metro*'s competition began to wither away. By 2012, total commuter daily circulation in the United Kingdom and Ireland had risen to 2.3 million from 300,000 in 1999, but London was the only market with more than one title (Bakker, 2013). *Metro* made money even during the recession, as Greenslade (2011) reported it 'made bumper profits in the 12 months up to October 2010 after enjoying years of money-making before that'.

> I wish I could tell you exactly how much it made, but the paper's publishers, Associated Newspapers, like to keep quiet about that. The profit is wrapped within the overall figures for the group. But it would not surprise me in the least if it made the best part of £30m in its last financial year and, quite possibly, even more.
>
> (Greenslade, 2011)

By 2016, the Metro franchise could claim to be the most-read newspaper in the United Kingdom with 10.4 million readers a month, up 9.5 percent year on year. Its digital edition, which was a facsimile of the print version designed to be read on tablets, claimed an average daily readership of just over 30,000, with an average time spent reading of 27 minutes, compared to 20 minutes for the average print newspaper. DMGT reported that *Metro*'s 2016 profit was £15 million on a turnover of £65 million, for a 23-percent profit margin, down from £16 million on a turnover of £70 million the previous year, largely because its editorial staff totalled only about 60. What made it attractive to advertisers was the average age of its readers, which at 37 was said to be 22 years younger than the print newspaper average (Ponsford, 2017, 24 March). In 2018, *Metro* surpassed the *Sun* in daily circulation with 1.5 million (Anonymous, 2018).

The afternoon commuter market saw only the *Evening Standard* survive. Its *Evening Lite* spinoff, which was renamed *London Lite* in 2006, was folded in 2009 after Lebedev bought the *Evening Standard*. He then made the long-publishing afternoon daily itself free, tripling its circulation and reviving its fortunes. The popularity of free newspapers ate into the sales of established newspapers, but the bursting of the advertising bubble with the recession hit them harder because they had no circulation revenue to fall back on. Almost half of the commuter dailies in Europe folded within five years and monopoly became the norm with typically only one free title in a market (Bakker, 2013). *Evening Standard* losses soon began to pile up, and between 2017 and 2022 they averaged £14 million a year (Sweney, 2022).

By 2020, national newspaper ownership concentration had far outstripped even the levels that drew concern from consecutive royal commissions. The Media Reform Coalition, which periodically recalculated concentration levels for its reports titled *Who Owns the UK Media?*, found that ownership by the three largest groups in 2020 had increased to almost 90 percent, as measured by combined daily and Sunday circulation, from 83 percent in 2018 and 71 percent in 2015 (Media Reform Coalition, 2015, 2019, 2021).

It also measured concentration by combined print and online reach, as well as by revenue, although the latter measure was complicated by the different reporting periods of publishers and by a rapidly changing ownership (Tables 4.1 and 4.2). As measured by revenue, national newspaper

Table 4.1 National newspaper weekly circulation (2020)

	Circulation	Share %	Cumulative
DMG Media	11,986,008	38.3	38.3
News UK	10,074,305	32.1	70.4
Reach	6,083,609	19.4	89.8
Telegraph	1,689,993	5.4	95.2
Guardian	842,691	2.7	97.9
Financial Times	652,851	2.1	100
	31,329,457		

Source: Media Reform Coalition, *Who Owns the UK media?* (2021)

Table 4.2 National newspaper market share by revenue (2019–20)

	Revenue (£m)	Share %	Cumulative	Reporting date
News UK	750	26.5	26.5	June 2019
DMG Media	672	23.7	50.2	Sept 2019
Reach	591	20.9	71.1	Dec 2019
Financial Times	345	12.2	83.3	Dec 2019
Telegraph	266	9.4	92.7	Dec 2019
Guardian	206	7.3	100	Mar 2020

Source: Media Reform Coalition, *Who Owns the UK media?* (2021)

concentration by the three largest groups had increased in two years from 61 percent to 71 percent. Total revenues in the industry increased slightly from £2.816 billion in its 2019 report to £2.83 billion.

Examining the financial data available on the Companies House website in more detail adds another dimension to this snapshot and provides a longitudinal portrait of newspaper industry health. The required filings of publishers allow their profitability to be calculated, albeit often with difficulty. Profitability importantly indicates sustainability, as newspapers have been found to be highly scalable because they can rapidly cut their costs in step with their revenues in order to remain profitable (Edge, 2014). The data available from Companies House show that newspapers remain profitable despite some down years recently and suggest that they are thus sustainable as a medium. In order to make comparisons, the standardised measure of EBITDA (earnings before interest, taxes, depreciation, and amortisation) has been calculated except where noted.

News Corp UK and Ireland

Untangling the financial fortunes of its UK, US, and Australian newspapers is impossible from reading News Corp's annual reports because they are lumped together in a division with its book publishers. The requirement of Companies House that all incorporated entities file annual financial statements, however, means that separate accounts must be submitted for company subsidiaries Times Newspapers and News Group Newspapers, the latter of which now includes only the *Sun* papers since closure of the *News of the World* in 2011. This allows for a more accurate picture to be drawn of how each of the company's national newspapers has performed over time.

News Group publishes the *Sun* and the *Sun on Sunday*. Its earnings, which fell to a loss for two years during the recession of 2008–09, had recovered by 2011 to a point where its profit margin reached 16.1 percent. Its closure of the *News of the World* that year dropped turnover only by about a quarter, as it soon commenced publishing the *Sun on Sunday*, which appealed to largely the same readership. Introduction of a paywall early in its 2014 fiscal year dropped digital revenues sharply, so it was lifted in late 2015, or midway through its 2016 fiscal year. A steep decline in print advertising, however, continued to drop its revenues. Revenues turned upward again in 2018–19 due to strong growth in digital advertising sales, but the onset of COVID-19 in early 2020 drastically dropped newsstand sales, on which the *Sun* relies heavily.

Table 4.3 News Group Newspapers Ltd.

	Turnover (£m)	EBITDA (£m)	Margin %
2005	657	61.1	9.3
2006	643	12.5	1.9
2007	623	10.7	1.7
2008	626	(18.5)	−2.9
2009	617	(15.5)	−2.5
2010	654	18.2	2.8
2011	654	105.3	16.1
2012*	509	16.2	3.2
2013	514	62.1	12.1
2014	489	35.6	7.3
2015	459	31.3	6.8
2016	446	16.1	3.6
2017	424	18.0	4.2
2018	401	12.8	3.2
2019	420	31.4	7.5
2020	324	2.3	0.7
2021	318	12.9	4.0

Year ended 30 June

*Closed *The News of the World* at beginning of fiscal year

Source: Companies House filings

The *Times* and the *Sunday Times* had long been prestigious loss leaders for Murdoch, but they have become quite profitable in recent years. As with most UK newspapers, their turnover dropped during the recession before stabilising. Key to the turnaround at the *Times* was introduction of its hard paywall in 2010. Cost-cutting also helped increase earnings to the point where by 2014 the *Times* newspapers were profitable for the first time in years. Turnover increased slightly in 2018 and 2019 but decreased significantly in 2020 due to declines in print circulation and print advertising sales. A combination of cost cuts, cover price increases, and increases in digital subscription and advertising sales, however, boosted earnings by half each of the past two years (Tables 4.3 and 4.4).

Table 4.4 Times Newspapers Ltd.

	Turnover (£m)	EBITDA (£m)	Margin %
2007	447	(34.2)	−7.6
2008	445	(42.7)	−9.6

(Continued)

Table 4.4 (Continued)

	Turnover (£m)	EBITDA (£m)	Margin %
2009	385	(71.9)	−18.6
2010	393	(42.4)	−10.8
2011	402	(9.5)	−2.4
2012	361	(13.4)	−3.7
2013	348	(5.9)	−1.7
2014	347	1.7	0.5
2015	345	21	6.1
2016	342	15.3	4.5
2017	319	7.0	2.2
2018	326	18.2	4.4
2019	330	14.7	5.6
2020	310	26.3	8.5
2021	327	52.5	16.0

Year ended 30 June
Source: Companies House filings

Associated Newspapers

This subsidiary of the Daily Mail and General Trust (DMGT) now owned by Lord Rothermere publishes the *Daily Mail*, the *Mail on Sunday*, MailOnline, *Metro*, and the *i*. It appears in DMGT's annual reports as its DMG Media division, but its segment share of company earnings is not reported. The company's reports to Companies House for Associated Newspapers, as DMGT's newspapers were formerly known, have thus been used instead (Table 4.5).

Table 4.5 Associated Newspapers

	Turnover (£m)	EBITDA (£m)	Margin %
2007	822	75.8	9.2
2008	834	63.0	7.5
2009	746	44.9	6.0
2010	726	73.7	10.1
2011	705	34.0	4.9
2012	715	51.1	7.2
2013	688	74.4	10.7
2014	679	51.3	7.1
2015	652	92.5	14.2
2016	650	76.9	11.8
2017	676	103.8	15.4
2018	652	59.6	9.1

	Turnover (£m)	EBITDA (£m)	Margin %
2019	656	89.8	13.7
2020	567	64.9	11.4

Year ending 30 September
Source: Companies House filings

Turnover dropped by just over 10 percent in 2009 as a result of the recession and eroded a few percent in most subsequent years, but it rose in 2017 after the *Daily Mail* made its first cover price increase in three years, from 60p to 65p, and also made about 200 layoffs (Williams, 2016). In late 2019, the company paid £50 million for the *i* newspaper, which had 2018 earnings of £11 million on revenues of £34 million. The COVID-19 pandemic contributed to a 26-percent decline in its 2019–20 print advertising revenues, but DMGT's 2021 annual report noted that its DMG Media division's revenues rose 3 percent, its operating profit rose 7 percent, and its operating margin was stable at 11 percent.

Reach plc

This listed company has been in expansion mode since selling Channel 5 to Viacom for £450 million in 2014 and buying the provincial publisher Local World for £183 million the following year. It was able to pay its first dividend for seven years in 2015 after its debt was reduced from £77.7 million to £19.3 million and its costs were cut by £15 million, but it became embroiled in the 2011 phone-hacking scandal and has had to set aside tens of millions of pounds to pay damage awards. It also has unfunded pension liabilities on the order of £300 million, reportedly as a result of mismanagement by former Mirror Group owner Robert Maxwell (Greenslade, 2015, 19 November).

Trinity Mirror reported separate results for its provincial and national newspapers until 2012, when they were combined. Turnover at its nationals fell by more than 10 percent as a result of the 2008–09 recession, but their earnings and profit margins remained strong as a result of cost-cutting, with its margin returning to 20 percent in 2010 (Tables 4.6 and 4.7).

The combined company, including local and regional titles, has been extremely profitable, with its margin exceeding 20 percent since 2012. Its revenues and earnings were boosted in 2016 by acquisition of the Local World chain, and in 2018 by acquisition of the Express group.

Table 4.6 Trinity Mirror Nationals

	Turnover (£m)	EBITDA (£m)	Margin %
2006	472	80.9	17.1
2007	488	94.3	19.3
2008	476	88.9	18.7
2009	460	83.6	18.2
2010	430	86.1	20.0
2011	453	83.1	18.2

Source: Companies House filings

Table 4.7 Trinity Mirror/Reach plc

	Turnover (£m)	EBITDA (£m)	Margin %
2012	616	125	20.3
2013	576	118.5	20.6
2014	554	113.5	20.5
2015*	529	114	21.5
2016	713	159.7	22.4
2017	623	145.1	23.3
2018**	724	167.9	23.2
2019	702	174.9	24.9
2020	600	161.2	26.9
2021	616	165.4	26.8

* Acquired Local World chain
** Acquired Express group
Source: Companies House filings

Telegraph Media Group

The company is a subsidiary of Press Holdings, which is owned by brothers David and Frederick Barclay, who also own the *Spectator* magazine. They acquired the group in 2004 following the shareholder-led implosion of Conrad Black's company Hollinger International. So robust were the Tely's operations that it maintained strong profit margins throughout the recession of 2008–09, after which they quickly increased to the high teens. The *Telegraph* was the UK's most profitable national newspaper for most of the 21st century until 2016, when its earnings fell by almost half. They again fell by a third in 2017 and by more half the following year. They have since recovered nicely, however, doubling in consecutive years before rising almost 8 percent in

2021, a full pandemic year, due to significant growth in digital subscription revenue (Table 4.8).

Table 4.8 Telegraph Media Group

	Turnover (£m)	EBITDA (£m)	Margin %
2006	341	32.7	9.6
2007	355	34.3	9.7
2008	343	32.0	9.3
2009	317	41.4	13.0
2010	324	60.1	18.6
2011	331	55.7	16.8
2012	327	58.4	17.8
2013	325	61.2	18.8
2014	318	54.9	17.3
2015	320	61.7	16.1
2016	295	32.2	10.9
2017	278	21.4	7.7
2018	271	7.8	2.9
2019	266	16.1	6.0
2020	235	37.5	15.9
2021	245	40.4	16.5

Source: Companies House filings

Financial Times

FT Publishing, which included the *Financial Times*, its website FT.com, and a half-interest in the *Economist*, was a division of education company Pearson before being sold (except for the *Economist* share) to Japanese company Nikkei in 2015. Until the mid-2000s, the *Financial Times* was in poor financial condition, losing tens of millions of pounds annually. An austerity programme and a refocusing on its digital operations turned that around by 2006. Its profits have since been driven by an increase in its digital revenues, which rose 40 percent in 2007 (Fine, 2008). It pioneered the 'metered' paywall that year, which would become the global industry standard. By 2008 its profits were going up while the rest of the industries were going down. An 80-percent cover price increase in print and 50-percent rise in its online price contributed to the increased profitability, as they were accompanied by only a 3-percent drop in readership (Hall, 2009). By 2016, the *Financial Times* saw a majority of its turnover from its digital operations and 60 percent of it from subscriptions (Greenslade, 2016) (Tables 4.9 and 4.10).

Table 4.9 Financial Times (Pearson)

	Turnover (£m)	Profit* (£m)	Margin %
2006	366	58	15.8
2007	344	56	16.3
2008	390	74	19.0
2009	358	39	10.9
2010	403	62	15.4
2011	427	76	17.8
2012	443	49	11.1
2013	341	29	8.5
2014	334	50	15.0
2015**	312	48	15.4

Source: Pearson plc annual reports

* As reported by Pearson

** Eleven months

Annual statements filed for the Financial Times with Companies House are remarkably opaque, claiming large annual losses by deducting from revenues unspecified charges listed only as 'Other'. Recourse was thus made to the annual reports of publicly traded Pearson plc, which proved more fulsome. Earnings for the FT Publishing Group did suffer a correction in 2009 with the recession, but by the following year they were growing again as its profit margin had returned to the mid-teens. This was seen until 2013, when turnover fell by more than £100 million. Earnings and margins both rebounded the following year, however. Since 2015, the financial statements filed with Companies House under ownership by Nikkei have proved more comprehensible. It is notable, however, that its reported earnings fell by about half immediately upon the change in ownership, perhaps as a result of management fees charged by the parent company.

Its accounts also now give only a partial view of the performance of the larger Financial Times Group because they cover only its main UK trading entity. The group incurs most of its costs in the United Kingdom but generates a large proportion of its revenues overseas (Mayhew, 2021). In 2015, the *Financial Times* switched from its metered paywall to a system of low-cost trials (Jackson & Plunkett, 2015). By 2017, it had 900,000 paying readers, including 700,000 online subscribers (Ponsford, 2017, 21 November). Its results for 2020 showed the impact of three pandemic lockdowns, as revenues fell 7 percent. Branded content sales rose 31 percent but failed to offset reduced print circulation sales (Mayhew, 2021). By 2022, paid subscriptions were up to 1.17 million, including 1 million online, only half of which were by UK residents.

Table 4.10 Financial Times (Nikkei)

	Turnover (£m)	EBITDA (£m)	Margin %
2016	310	23.1	7.5
2017	321	22.7	7.1
2018	323	27.7	8.6
2019	345	36.1	10.5
2020	319	10.0	3.1

Source: Companies House filings

The Guardian

The Guardian Media Group, which publishes the *Guardian*, the Sunday *Observer*, and the website Guardian Online, is an anomaly among UK newspaper publishers in that it is owned by the Scott Trust and its losses are thus underwritten by a rich endowment. Attention to cost-cutting under falling revenues was thus not as urgent as at other national dailies. The *Guardian* has also bet big on digital journalism, keeping its website free while other publishers were erecting paywalls to recoup needed revenues (Table 4.11).

Table 4.11 Guardian Media Group

	Turnover (£m)	EBITDA (£m)	Margin %
2007	245.7	(6.0)	−2.4
2008	261.9	(4.1)	−1.5
2009	253.6	7.5	2.9
2010	221.0	(15.5)	−7.0
2011	198.2	(20.1)	−10.1
2012	196.2	(32.2)	−16.3
2013	208.8	(40.9)	−19.6
2014	210.2	(17.8)	−8.5
2015	214.7	(40.5)	−18.8
2016	209.5	(68.7)	−32.8
2017	214.5	(44.7)	−20.8
2018	217.0	(23.0)	−10.6
2019	224.5	(3.7)	−1.6
2020	223.5	(6.9)	−3.0
2021	225.5	12.4	0.5
2022	255.8	20.7	8.1

Year ending 31 March
Source: Companies House filings

The digital bet looked like a losing one, at least financially, as online advertising revenues stagnated and print losses mounted. The *Guardian*'s investment fund also fell to an estimated £740 million by 2016 due to a downturn in financial markets (Glover, 2016). As a result of its losses, the *Guardian* announced an austerity programme in 2016 designed to cut costs by 20 percent, or just over £50 million, in a bid to break even within three years (Martinson, 2016, 25 January). In early 2016 it made 250 job cuts, including 100 in editorial (Martinson, 2016, 17 March) and a cover price increase of 20p came the following month (Sweney, 2016, 9 May). It suffered a record annual loss of £68.7 million for its fiscal year ended in the spring of 2016 but reported that more than 50,000 readers had signed up for 'memberships' which it hoped would increase revenues by more than £30 million (Jackson, 2016). In early 2017, the *Guardian* announced it had 200,000 paying members, which *Press Gazette* estimated could be contributing around £10 million a year to its bottom line. A further 160,000 readers had made one-time contributions, *Guardian* editor Katharine Viner disclosed, which helped offset advertising losses of £11 million (Ponsford, 2017, 17 March). By November 2021, it announced that it had more than 1 million paying readers from 180 countries, most of whom lived outside the United Kingdom, including 419,541 digital subscriptions and 580,494 recurring contributions (Anonymous, 2021). The support from its readers helped Guardian Media Group record a profit of £12.4 million for its 2020–21 fiscal year, its first in years.

Note

1. return on capital

5 The Provincial Press

The Problem of Free

The contrast between the UK's national press and its local and regional newspaper industry could hardly be more marked. While the national dailies and Sunday newspapers compete vigorously, an industry tendency towards monopoly was ensconced long ago at the provincial level. The advertising boom which began in the 1950s created an enormous market to exploit outside London, where local and regional newspapers surpassed the nationals in readership. Since people shopped close to home, provincial publishers became eager to gather audiences they could in turn sell to advertisers. The number of local and regional titles published in the United Kingdom has historically been difficult to determine, noted Ramsay and Moore (2016), due to the lack of a central reporting source. The number of provincial newspapers peaked in about 1900, according to Curran (2003), when there were 196 local dailies and 2072 weeklies. Those numbers fell by 1920 to 169 and 1700, respectively, 'due mainly to the casualties caused by intense competition' (Curran, 2003, p. 32). At the same time, noted Matthews (2015, p. 243), 'circulations – and profits – increased, making this a battle worth fighting'.

Chains of local weeklies had been formed by industrialists as early as the 18th century, and chains of local dailies such as the one controlled by Andrew Carnegie emerged shortly after the explosion of titles brought by the lifting of taxes on knowledge in 1855. The chains that would dominate the 20th century, however, were formed mostly in the 1920s. Allied Newspapers was founded in 1924 by the Berry brothers, a/k/a Lord Kemsley and Viscount Camrose, and grew by 1939 to include 20 daily and Sunday papers (Curran, 2003). Allied acquired the *Daily Telegraph* in 1928 but the company was split in 1937, with the provincial titles being retained by Lord Kemsley in a company named after him. Lord Rothermere, owner of the *Daily Mail*, founded Associated Newspapers in 1928 and became,

DOI: 10.4324/9780429469206-6

according to Matthews (2017, p. 122), 'perhaps the most notorious accelerator of efforts to consolidate ownership'.

> His bid to create a national chain of evening newspapers set a standard for aggressive marketing techniques and sowed disquiet among members of the industry, who fought to oppose his quest for domination. Rothermere was reported to have been driven by a wish to be the largest newspaper proprietor in the country after the ascendancy of Allied Newspapers.
>
> (Matthews, 2017, pp. 122–123)

The result, according to Curran (2003, p. 32), was 'a long-drawn-out and costly' battle between the Berry brothers and Rothermere 'which was eventually resolved in a series of local treaties in which the three lords divided up different parts of the country between them'. Battleground markets included Bristol and Newcastle, where Rothermere founded evening newspapers in 1929 to compete with entrenched Berry dailies. Within a few years the intense competition prompted a truce, according to a 1938 government study. 'In 1932 the position had become so serious that a pact was fixed up whereby the Harmsworth interests retired from Newcastle and the Berry interests from Bristol, and incidentally from Derby as well' (Political and Economic Planning, 1938, pp. 59–60).

> The 'war' in Bristol, however, was not yet over. A body of Bristol citizens, resenting this invasion of their city by a monopolistic outside concern, set up in 1932 the *Bristol Evening Post* in rivalry to the *Bristol Evening World*. The conflict eventually proved so expensive to both sides that in January 1936 a fresh truce was reached, by which both newspapers came under one ownership, Bristol United Press Ltd., 75 per cent of the shares of which are owned by Associated Newspapers.
>
> (Political and Economic Planning, 1938, p. 60)

The result, noted Matthews (2017), was that a city which in 1928 had four newspapers soon had only one. A similar outcome was seen in Leicester, noted Fowler (2011), after Rothermere entered that market in 1931 with the *Evening Mail* and competed aggressively against the locally owned *Evening Mercury*. A truce was called in 1939 when the newspapers entered into a partnership, which Associated took over in 1954, closing the *Evening Mail* in 1963. 'Such wheeling and dealing would be unthinkable today', noted Fowler (2011, p. 15). 'Probably illegal, too'. Matthews (2017) noted that while there were 41 provincial morning dailies and 89 evening dailies in 1921, those numbers had dropped by 1937 to 28 and 75. 'Local monopoly had become the dominant order of the day for the provincial newspaper' (Matthews, 2017, p. 114).

> In most cities titles were in monopoly positions due not only to competition but also to inter-group cooperation, which saw areas delimited between them. This is perhaps due to the nature of the profitability of the evening newspaper, which did not need ever-increasing sales, but instead found its profitability in the amount it could charge for advertising.
>
> (Matthews, 2017, pp. 119–120)

Commercially motivated owners, she added, consolidated their positions by buying multiple titles to create monopolistic business models with defined circulation areas. The industry thus became dominated by a few huge enterprises. 'Between 1921 and 1946 these groups increased their total holding of titles from just under 15 per cent of total titles to nearly 43 per cent' (Matthews, 2015, p. 243). 'Best equipped were those large companies who could resource costly circulation wars, often via the evening paper – a highly refined and profitable commercial product' (Matthews, 2015, p. 243). According to Matthews (2017, p. 168), the increasingly consolidated newspaper industry 'enabled provincial newspaper owners to negotiate monopolistic circulation areas so they could fully exploit finite advertising markets'.

The 1949 Royal Commission on the Press, however, all but dismissed the problem of ownership concentration in the provincial newspaper industry. It noted that the chains had grown more slowly during the 1930s than in the previous decade and that there was even a tendency from 1937 onward for concentration to abate. 'In comparison with other undertakings chains were in no stronger a position in 1946 than in 1937. There is no reason to expect that the aggressive expansion which characterised their early phase will be resumed' (RCTP, 1949, p. 93). While it found a monopoly in 58 of the 66 towns which had a daily newspaper, the report concluded: 'Many of the 58 towns in which local monopoly occurs are clearly too small to support more than one paper' (RCTP, 1949, p. 98). Concentration of local weekly newspaper ownership, the report added, was 'negligible' (RCTP, 1949, p. 175). Only in provincial dailies did the chains have an undesirable number or proportion of titles, it found, and in that field there were still 41 separate owners. The five largest chains together owned 44 percent of the morning papers and 63 percent of the evenings. Kemsley, the largest had 24 percent of the morning papers and 12 percent of the evenings. 'These proportions are high, but in terms of numbers the concentration has not increased significantly since 1929 and in terms of circulation it decreased between 1937 and 1947' (RCTP, 1949, p. 98).

> In the provincial Press as a whole there is nothing approaching monopoly and we see no strong tendency towards monopoly. The degree of concentration in the provincial Press is considerable, but not in our view so great as in itself to prejudice the free expression of opinion and the accurate presentation of news, or to be contrary to the best interests of the public.
>
> (RCTP, 1949, p. 98)

By the time the second Royal Commission on the Press convened a dozen years later, the three largest provincial chains – the Daily Mirror group, Associated Newspapers, and Beaverbrook Newspapers – had increased their share of circulation from 45 percent to 67 percent. 'There is now no town in England or Wales with more than one entirely locally published morning newspaper', its report noted. 'In Glasgow there are two and in Belfast three. In only seven towns outside London are there more than one evening newspaper, and in four of these towns the evening newspapers are under common ownership' (Royal Commission on the Press, 1962, p. 17). Then in 1963 a wave of closures hit the regional evening press, with papers shut down in Birmingham, Nottingham, Manchester, Leicester, Leeds, and Edinburgh, leaving those cities with only one evening daily each (Williams, 2010). According to Temple (2017, p. 97): 'Competition between evening papers in England's major cities effectively ended in 1963, when the poor advertising revenue of the *Manchester Evening Chronicle* led to a merger with the *Manchester Evening News*, effectively establishing a regional monopoly for the latter.' The lucrative evening monopoly gained by the *News* helped to subsidise the losses of its sister newspaper, the morning *Guardian*, which began national distribution and moved to Fleet Street in 1961 (Rusbridger, 2018).

Provincial press monopolies soon drew competition for their lucrative advertising revenues from free newspapers. The concept was imported from Australia by former sports reporter Lionel Pickering, who founded the *Derby Trader* in 1966 and within twenty years had built a chain of ten profitable titles. The genre spread rapidly, with 9.4 million copies of free newspapers circulating a week by 1974, compared to 11.2 million copies of paid weeklies (Matthews, 2017). The freesheets, Matthews noted, benefited from new computer technology which enabled them to be produced with fewer staff. 'They were typically run by just three or four people, yet offered blanket coverage of an area to advertisers' (Matthews, 2017, p. 177) Established newspaper companies in response increased their investment in freesheets (Matthews, 2017, p. 177). 'Westminster Press Ltd, for instance, published twelve free titles in 1977, eleven of which had been launched since 1971'. According to Hill (2016, p. 37), the free newspaper phenomenon 'exposed a vulnerability in the newspaper doctrine that the newspaper industry was protected by high entry barriers'. By contracting out their printing and running minimal editorial operations, the freesheets avoided having to make the huge capital investments in printing presses and large staffs which were traditionally needed to start a newspaper. Pickering, for example, founded the *Derby Trader* with just £4,800 in capital, operating it initially out of his mother's house and writing, designing, and even distributing the paper himself (Matthews, 2017).

The third Royal Commission on the Press noted a drop in the number of freesheets to about 130 in 1976 as a result of an ongoing recession, compared with 150 in 1974. This included about 40 which had been started by local authorities and were published bi-monthly or quarterly. While it found freesheets an 'interesting phenomenon', the Royal Commission doubted their staying power.

> Our evidence suggests that it is difficult to establish a freesheet with any expectation of long life. . . . We do not accept therefore that the existence of freesheets is particularly strong evidence that new publishers can successfully create a long term alternative to existing weekly newspapers.
>
> (RCTP, 1977a, p. 55)

As part of its inquiry, the third Royal Commission ordered a report on ownership concentration in the provincial press. It found that freesheet circulation had grown from 2.3 million in 1970 to 9.4 million at the height of the 1973–74 advertising boom but declined with the ensuing recession to 5.9 million in 1976.

> Many freesheets have had a fleeting existence, and a number come and go without becoming established in the market. However, a number of titles have lasted longer but they constitute less than 10 percent of the titles observed over the period as a whole.
>
> (RCTP, 1977b, p. 88)

It cited Advertising Association estimates that freesheet revenue had grown from £1 million in 1968 to £18 million by 1975, mostly from a boom in classifieds, or from 2 percent that of paid weeklies to 20 percent.

> Freesheets have in many areas been able to mount an effective challenge to the existing weekly publishers, though they did best when

advertising expenditure was expanding very rapidly and many existing papers found it difficult to expand sufficiently to meet the demand.

(RCTP, 1977b, p. 91)

The report cited a number of observers who argued that freesheets were 'at best a marginal advertising medium, or prosper only under favourable local conditions' (RCTP, 1977b, p. 91).

Where a local newspaper is able to take up the demand for advertising space satisfactorily, then advertisers have a strong preference for using them. No evidence has emerged of any paid-for weekly paper closing as a result of competition from a freesheet.

(RCTP, 1977b, p. 91)

While the Royal Commission found that there had been only a moderate increase in ownership concentration of provincial dailies, it noted a steep drop in the number of weekly newspaper owners, to 180 from 460 in 1961 (RCTP, 1977a). The percentage of weeklies owned by chains had more than doubled between 1961 and 1974, it noted, largely as a result of acquisitions. The increase in concentration of ownership in all categories of provincial newspaper was mostly a regional phenomenon, the Royal Commission added.

Companies which have acquired newspapers have generally done so in an area where they already had newspaper interests. In addition, they have launched new newspapers in these areas. Increasingly large geographical groupings of newspapers owned by one company have been the result.

(RCTP, 1977a, p. 25)

Westminster Press, for example, expanded mainly in the North, North and West Yorkshire, and the South. In the North, where it owned four of the ten dailies published, it increased its share of weekly circulation from 43 percent in 1961 to 55 percent in 1974. News UK owned both evening newspapers and 'virtually all' of the weeklies in Hereford and Worcester. The Liverpool Daily Post and Echo Limited both owned daily papers in Merseyside and published almost 60 percent of weekly newspaper circulation there (RCTP, 1977a).

The economies of scale available from multi-title publishing were so large, noted the Royal Commission, that the chains were willing to pay premium prices for strategic acquisitions. 'One measure of this is that firms have been prepared to acquire weekly newspaper companies for sums equivalent to 20–30 times post-tax profits, which is a high price by the standards of other businesses' (RCTP, 1977a, p. 52). Chain expansion had been fueled by a boom in advertising revenues, it found, which had more than tripled at provincial newspapers from £77 million in 1960 to £282 million by 1975. The national chains had pushed their profit margins from 20 percent in 1972 to 23 percent in 1973 before they slumped with the recession to 15 percent in 1974 (RCTP, 1977a). 'Except for morning newspapers, a few of which are in danger of closure, the provincial press is generally very profitable. This is because much of it operates in monopoly conditions' (RCTP, 1977a, pp. 73–74).

Despite the Royal Commission's skepticism, the rapid growth in freesheets resumed once the 1974–75 recession ended. Their number grew to 1000 by 1980, when they formed their own trade group, the Association of Free Newspapers (Hill, 2016). 'This was not a newspaper form to be easily dismissed', noted Matthews (2017, p. 119), 'and their growth was to accelerate in the 1980s to a peak circulation of 42 million in 1989'. Chain ownership also increased, driven by new entrants to the market. Reed Regional Newspapers, a subsidiary of paper maker Reed International, published 100 freesheets by 1991 with a total circulation of 5.8 million, and in 1984 even launched a free daily, the *Birmingham Daily News*, which at its peak employed about 40 journalists (Matthews, 2017). Distributing more than 320,000 copies to 86 percent of homes, it soon claimed 25 percent of Birmingham's advertising revenue (Franklin & Murphy, 1991).

By the late 1980s, free newspapers outnumbered paid, as *Benn's Directory* counted 931 freesheets in 1988, compared to 797 paid weeklies and 70 dailies (Franklin & Murphy, 1991). Their advertising revenues soared to £405 million in 1987, a 29-percent increase from the previous year. While regional newspaper advertising revenues rose 49 percent overall from 1982–87, noted Franklin and Murphy (1991), they rose by only 34 percent for dailies and 24 percent for paid weeklies. At free newspapers, however, they jumped 132 percent. 'The rate and significance of free newspaper growth cannot . . . be overstated', concluded Franklin and Murphy (1991, p. 7). They pointed out that increased competition from freesheets not only depressed the circulation of paid weeklies, which dropped by 35 percent from 1977 to 1987, but also constrained them from raising their cover prices, which dropped their revenues from sales to only 14 percent of total revenues (Franklin & Murphy, 1991). The result, they found, was a trend towards commercialisation of the regional press. In order to cut costs, the paid weeklies increasingly adopted the shoestring editorial content model favoured by the freesheets, which consisted mostly of press releases and paid advertorials.

Dizzying changes were seen by the 1990s, according to Clark (2017, p. 59), as the surviving independent groups and titles 'were almost all picked off and gobbled up by bigger regional publishers'. Pickering sold out to Thomson in 1989 and Thomson in turn sold its provincial newspapers to the Trinity chain in 1995. In 1996 alone, ownership of one-third of all regional newspaper companies changed hands (Franklin & Murphy, 1998). Trinity merged with the Mirror Group in 1999 to form Trinity Mirror and embarked on an expansion. Reed Regional was taken over in a management buyout to form Newsquest, which was bought by Gannett in 1999 and soon acquired Westminster Press from Pearson. Newsquest also won a bidding war the following year with Johnston Press for News Communications & Media, the eighth-largest UK regional newspaper chain, paying £444 million for its 99 titles, including four dailies. Newsquest then bought the *Glasgow Herald*, the *Sunday Herald*, and the *Evening Times*, along with 11 magazines, from the Scottish Media Group in 2003 for £216 million (Franklin, 2006). The Norwich-based Archant chain bought 27 weeklies from Independent News & Media in 2004 (Johnson, 2004).

By 2005, the number of companies publishing local newspapers had dropped to 87 from 137 in 1998 and 200 in 1992, and by 2006 the top four groups – Trinity Mirror, Johnston Press, Newsquest, and DMGT – owned 65 percent of all regional titles (Matthews, 2017). Their expansionism was fueled by soaring advertising revenues, which within a decade rose more than a thousandfold, from £2.7 million in 1995 to more than £3 billion in 2004 (Franklin, 2006). Increased revenues and the economies achieved by consolidation drove profits even higher, noted Matthews (2017, p. 192). 'Profit margins of between 24 and 30 per cent were not unusual for the regional newspaper industry in 2004 and could reach as much as 40 per cent'.

The boom in provincial advertising revenues attracted the attention of investors, and as the bubble inflated, it only served to fuel corporate expectations. As Clark (2017, p. 66) noted: 'The regional press went from a business which thought it was ambitious to have margins of 20 per cent, to one which enjoyed margins of up to 50 per cent in just ten years between the mid-1990s and the mid-2000s'. Soon local newspapers began changing hands at an even more rapid pace, noted Matthews (2017, p. 172). 'Titles were shifted between the largest newspapers groups as each jockeyed for dominance, and this often brought widespread disruption for those on the ground'. Among the titles that changed hands more than once was Britain's oldest continuously published newspaper, the weekly *Stamford Mercury*. It was bought in 1929 by Westminster Press and managed jointly with its *Lincolnshire Chronicle*, according to Matthews (2017, p. 172). 'Printing was removed from Stamford, the title was redesigned and then merged with surrounding weekly titles when they too were bought'. It was sold in 1951 to East Midland Allied Press (EMAP), which had been formed by the merger of four newspaper publishers in the east of England. The *Mercury* changed hands again in 1996, when EMAP was acquired by Johnston Press, and again in 2017 when Johnston sold it and 12 other titles to Iliffe Media.

With the advent of the World Wide Web, some chains decided like Reed to sell off their newspaper holdings. Thomson not only sold to Trinity in 1995 and got out of the United Kingdom but also divested its worldwide newspaper empire almost entirely. By early in the new millennium it had sold off all of its newspaper holdings, which had once included 233 titles in North America and 151 in the United Kingdom, except for the national *Globe and Mail* in its native Canada. Instead of news, it bet big on information, acquiring electronic database companies in the United States, often for billions of dollars (Krekhovetsky, 2003). Following the 2006 death of company head Ken Thomson, a third generation of family ownership bought the historic Reuters news service in 2008 and moved it to Toronto as Thomson Reuters. Their move out of newspapers proved prescient, as the Internet was about to diminish them severely.

The frenzy of newspaper acquisitions soon began to slow with a credit crunch, and it ended abruptly with a stock market crash which ushered in the recession of 2008–09. According to Matthews (2017, p. 195), a 'wake-up call' had come in 2005 when DMGT was unable to sell its regional division Northcliffe Newspapers, rejecting an offer of £1.1 billion. Archant suffered a drop in profit that year of more than 12 percent due to the flight of recruitment and auto advertising online (Matthews, 2017). Other chains continued to buy, however, ignoring the growing impact that the Internet was having on news consumption. Johnston Press bought eight Scottish titles from Archant in 2007, giving it 315 local and regional newspapers, including 18 dailies (Nel, 2013). By 2012, that had fallen by 28 percent due to divestitures to 13 daily and 214 weekly papers while its staff numbers were nearly halved from 7,538 to 3,960. The recession and bursting of the post-war advertising bubble re-shaped the industry into a form that would have been barely recognisable a decade earlier, noted Fowler (2011, p. 25).

> In the twelve years from 1995 to 2007 four of the five major groups of the 1990s – Thomson Regional Newspapers, Westminster Press, United Provincial Newspapers, and Reed Regional Newspapers – had largely disappeared to be replaced by the groups that had acquired and merged in an aggressive fashion – Trinity Mirror, Johnston Press, and Newsquest.

Ownership of the provincial press was even more highly concentrated by 2021, with the three largest firms controlling 61.9 percent of titles, a level the MRC (2021, p. 3) deemed 'dangerous'. Newsquest's 2022 acquisition of Archant brought that to 69 percent. The MRC's (2021) compilation of regional press ownership concentration has been modified to reflect that acquisition (Table 5.1).

Table 5.1 Local newspapers by publisher (2022)

	Titles	Share %	Cumulative
Newsquest	308	30.3	30.3
Reach	211	20.7	51.0
JPI Media	183	18.0	69.0
Tindle	79	7.8	76.8
Iliffe Media	71	7.0	83.8
Remaining 50 Publishers	166	19.1	100.00
Total	1018		

Source: Media Reform Coalition, Who Owns the UK media? (2021)

Newsquest

Newsquest has been in acquisition mode for years, undeterred by the Great Recession or even the Internet, growing from 186 titles in 2013 to 236 in 2021 before adding Archant's 72 titles the following year to give it 308 (Media Reform Coalition, 2014, 2021). Most were weeklies, both paid and free, but Newsquest also published 22 dailies, including the *Glasgow Herald, Northern Echo, Bradford Telegraph & Argus, Southampton Southern Daily Echo, Brighton Argus, Oxford Mail*, and *South Wales Argus*. The company was a subsidiary of Gannett, the largest US chain, which had a reputation for rapacious growth and aggressive cost-cutting (Weiss, 1987; McCord, 2001; Stephens, 2015). That was before it was acquired in 2018 by the hedge fund Fortress Investment Group. Perhaps not surprisingly, Newsquest has come under criticism in the United Kingdom for the same tactics. It bought the Carlisle-based CN Group in 2018, which consisted of the evening daily *News and Star* and a half-dozen smaller titles. Roger Lytollis, a journalist who was made redundant by Newsquest, noted that while CN had cut its staff in the previous few years, Newsquest took this to 'spectacular' levels. 'Its six papers in Cumbria now have no photographers, no sub-editors, no feature writers and one sports journalist' (Lytollis, 2021).

In the depths of the 2008–09 recession, the company's Herald and Times Group in Scotland made all of its 250 journalists and publishing staff redundant and then invited them to reapply for their jobs with the promise to re-hire only 220 who agreed to wage cuts (Bolger, 2008). One of Newsquest's strategies was to buy up neighbouring titles and move them to a regional 'production hub' with a barebones staff. When it bought the family-owned *Richmond and Twickenham Times* in 2001, for example, it slashed its staff and moved the weekly to Sutton, ten miles away, where 18 employees put out no fewer than 11 titles (Preston, 2016).

When Newsquest announced profits of £69.1 million for 2014, up 2.7 percent from the year before, its filing with Companies House revealed that it was a result of 228 staff having been cut that year, reducing its headcount to 3,997 and cutting its costs by more than £5 million. The filing also showed that remuneration of Newsquest directors had topped £1 million for the first time, while their bonus payments increased by £338,000 and Newsquest's CEO was paid more than £400,000 (Sweney, 2015). The revelations prompted a series of strikes at Newsquest titles across the United Kingdom in 2015 to protest job cuts and poor pay, including one at its London and south-east operations that lasted for ten days (Connelly, 2015).

It was the first time that Newsquest's annual filing with Companies House had reported consolidated results for the entire group, which was made up of more than two dozen subsidiaries. The company switched accounting standards the following year and also took advantage of provisions in the Companies Act which exempted it from reporting group cash flow. Its annual filings thus became more opaque, but Newsquest's overall performance could still be inferred by examining filings for its subsidiaries. The results for the two largest, which together comprised almost half of the company's 2014 revenues, show that Newsquest continued to be a very profitable enterprise.

'Newsquest Media (Southern)

Judging from its 2014 turnover, this subsidiary contributed about 25 percent of Newsquest's revenues. Turnover fell by one-third from 2006 to 2009, then eroded more slowly. Profit margins, which had been in excess of 30 percent before the recession, remained strong at greater than 20 percent from 2008 to 2012 but fell in 2013 before rebounding. In 2015, the London Assembly passed a motion urging then-mayor Boris Johnson to protest to Newsquest its staff cutbacks and the relocation of jobs outside London (Greenslade, 2015, 2 December). The subsidiary was folded into Newsquest Media Group Limited at the end of 2016 (Tables 5.2–5.4).

Table 5.2 Newsquest Media Group Limited

	Turnover (£m)	EBITDA (£m)	Margin %
2013	288	67.3	23.3
2014	279	69.1	24.8

Source: Companies House filings

Table 5.3 Newsquest Media (Southern) Limited

	Turnover (£m)	EBITDA (£m)	Margin%
2006	129	42.8	33.1
2007	128	40.6	31.5
2008	110	31.6	28.6
2009	86	18.6	21.5
2010	85	20.7	24.5
2011	81	23.5	29.1
2012	75	16.8	22.4
2013	72	8.2	11.5
2014	69	13.7	19.7
2015	64	11.2	17.7
2016*	57	2.4	4.3

* Company reorganised 26 December 2016
Source: Companies House filings

Table 5.4 Newsquest (Herald & Times) Limited

	Turnover (£m)	EBITDA (£m)	Margin %
2006	88	22.9	25.9
2007	87	21.8	25.1
2008	79	21.4	26.9
2009	63	12.0	19.0
2010	58	10.4	17.9
2011	57	11.2	19.6
2012	57	14.7	25.8
2013	54	12.1	22.5
2014	55	14.8	27.6
2015	52	12.9	25.0
2016	45	8.2	18.3
2017*	43	10.6	24.7

* Company reorganised 31 December 2017
Source: Companies House filings

This subsidiary contributed about 20 percent of Newsquest's 2014 revenues. It published the morning *Glasgow Herald* and evening *Glasgow Times* along with the *Sunday Herald* and the Scottish daily *The National*, which began publishing in 2014. Its results over the past decade show the same trend of plummeting revenues during the recession of 2008–09 and their steady erosion ever since. Earnings were cut by more than half before rebounding in 2012. They dropped sharply again in 2013, however, before rising as a result of cost-cutting. Four rounds of redundancies starting in 2015 saw 25 journalists leave, with another 20 severed in early 2016, leaving an estimated 100 remaining and bringing a union warning that 'unrealistic profit targets' posed a 'serious risk to future of the newspapers in this stable' (BBC, 2016). At the end of 2017, this subsidiary was also folded into Newsquest Media Group Limited (Table 5.5).

Table 5.5 Newsquest Media Group Limited

	Turnover (£m)	EBITDA (£m)	Margin %
2017	130	21.3	16.2
2018	197	34.5	17.5
2019	187	38.3	20.3
2020	139	32.3	23.1
2021	142	35.6	25.1

Source: Companies House filings

By 2018, all but a few of Newsquest's subsidiaries, which together comprised less than 10 percent of its 2014 revenues, had been folded into the parent company. This allowed for a much better picture of the company's overall financial health to be drawn from its results. Steady declines in turnover continued to be seen, but its earnings remained strong and its profit margins steadily increased.

Reach Plc

Ownership of Reach is held mostly by institutional investors. Its largest shareholders are the UK-based firms M&G plc (12 percent), Aberforth Partners (10 percent), and Premier Miton Group (5 percent). It has been in both expansion and contraction modes during the past decade, not only closing and consolidating marginal titles but also acquiring other groups in order to regain lost scale. In 2010, Trinity Mirror acquired the 22 regional titles of GMG's MEN Media subsidiary for £44.8 million, including the *Manchester Evening News* and the *Reading Evening Post*. Following the £463 million sale of its Channel 5 in 2014, it bought the recently formed Local World chain, of which it already owned 20 percent, for £220 million. The 83 titles it thus acquired briefly made Trinity Mirror the largest publisher of UK provincial newspapers before it was surpassed by Newsquest.

Trinity Mirror's corporate financial statements were often more forthcoming than its more opaque filings with Companies House. Changes in the company's reporting practices, however, make longitudinal comparisons problematic. Until 2011, for example, Trinity Mirror reported results separately for its nationals and its provincial titles, but it then combined them. Its more than 200 provincial newspapers regularly generated even higher profit margins than its nationals until the recession of 2008–09, but they did not prove as robust through the economic downturn (see Chapter 4). Their margins were in excess of 20 percent until the recession of 2008–09, when they briefly dropped below 10 percent before rebounding into the teens (Tables 5.6 and 5.7).

Table 5.6 Trinity Mirror Regionals

	Turnover (£m)	EBITDA(£m)	Margin %
2006	531	118.1	22.2
2007	484	112.6	23.2
2008	396	60.9	15.4
2009	303	28.8	9.5
2010	331	51.7	15.6
2011	294	36.5	12.4

Source: Trinity Mirror plc annual reports

Table 5.7 Reach Regionals Media Limited

	Turnover (£m)	EBITDA (£m)	Margin %
2015	16.6	6.4	38.5
2016	108	17.9	16.5
2017	124	24.0	19.3
2018	197	31.4	15.9
2019	178	26.2	14.7
2020	143	29.3	20.5
2021	157	30.3	19.3

Source: Companies House filings

Trinity Mirror North West & North Wales Limited, a subsidiary which once included only Trinity's original *Liverpool Echo*, its *Daily Post* in North Wales, and several weeklies, grew with the addition of its Media Wales subsidiary, along with 22 local and regional titles acquired from the Guardian Media Group in 2010. It then gained more than 100 titles acquired in Trinity Mirror's £220 million acquisition of Local World in 2015, including the *Bristol Post*. After growing twelvefold in turnover, the subsidiary became Reach Regionals Media Limited in 2018 as part of a corporate rebranding. It recorded profit margins in the mid-teens from 2016 onward that topped 20 percent in 2020 despite falling revenues during the pandemic.

JPIMedia

Johnston Press provides a cautionary tale of newspaper business peril in rapidly changing times. The Scottish publisher was founded in 1764 as a printing company and expanded into publishing in 1846 with the acquisition of several weekly newspapers. It grew to 24 titles in 1974 and went public in 1988, selling shares on the London Stock Exchange. It paid £29.4 million for its first daily, the *Halifax Courier*, and its nine-newspaper group in 1994. It soon embarked on what Nel (2013, p. 7) described as 'an extraordinary succession of takeovers', growing by 2007 to 315 titles, then the most of any publisher in the United Kingdom. Its rise was meteoric, as it had only become the UK's fifth largest local and regional publisher in 1996 when it bought the 65-title chain EMAP for £111 million. It added the rival Portsmouth & Sunderland chain in 1999 for £266 million, boosting Johnston Press from 155 titles to more than 200 and fourth place among local and regional publishers. It bought 14 titles, including the *Lincoln Standard*, from Southnews for £16.5 million in 2000 and added the 53-title Regional Independent Media, and then the UK's fifth largest chain and owner of the *Yorkshire Post*, for £560 million in 2002.

In the last six months of 2005 alone, Johnston spent more than £500 million on acquisitions, including £155 million for 35 titles from Scottish Radio Holdings and £65 million for the Local Press Group, whose dozen titles included the daily *Belfast News Letter*. The £155 million it spent to buy the five Irish titles of Score Press, and the £95 million it paid for the Leinster Leader Group of six dailies and weeklies made Johnston Press the largest newspaper publisher in the Republic (Cawley, 2017). Before the year was out, Johnston also bought Scotsman Publications, including *The Scotsman, Scotland on Sunday*, and the *Edinburgh Evening News*.

By 2007, the company had assets approaching £2 billion and annual revenues exceeding £600 million. Its profit margin was 35 percent, and its stock traded at a high of £4.90. Unfortunately for Johnston Press, it picked the very top of the market to expand so ambitiously. Revenues fell across the regional newspaper industry in 2006, with the top groups suffering drops averaging 6.4 percent led by declines of 16–17 percent in job ad revenues and 15–17 in car ad sales (Press Gazette, 2007). They went into freefall with the onset of recession in 2007 and would eventually drop by half between 2004 and 2011, from £3 billion to about £1.5 billion (Gulyas, 2012).

Johnston Press cut costs by laying off staff, closing titles, and converting five of its 19 dailies to weeklies. It hiked cover prices aggressively to increase revenues, but resisted putting paywalls up around its online content. It sold off assets to pay down debt, divesting entire divisions for a fraction of what they had been acquired for. It bought the national commuter daily *i* for £24 million in 2016 when its parent *Independent* went online-only, and its profits of £1 million a month helped keep Johnston Press afloat for two more years. In the end, however, Johnston Press could not outrun its debt. It entered bankruptcy proceedings in 2018 and was taken over by a consortium of its creditors led by GoldenTree Asset Management, a US hedge fund (Table 5.8).

Table 5.8 Johnston Press

	Turnover (£m)	EBITDA (£m)	Margin %	Debt (£m)
2006	602	186.8	31.0	753
2007	607	178.1	29.3	688
2008	532	128.4	24.1	518
2009	428	71.8	16.8	429
2010	398	72.0	18.1	400
2011	374	64.6	17.3	372
2012	329	57.0	17.4	342
2013	292	54.3	18.6	323
2014	266	55.5	20.9	215
2015	242	57.3	23.7	186
2016	222	49.1	22.1	143
2017	201	40.1	19.9	166

Source: Companies House filings

Renamed JPIMedia, its new owners first sold the *i* to DMGT for £49.4 million, or more than twice what Johnston Press had paid for it. They then sold the rest of JPIMedia at the end of 2018 to a new company named National World for £10.2 million. National World put paywalls up around JPIMedia's online content and expanded with online publications in seven new markets, including Glasgow, Liverpool, Birmingham, Bristol, Manchester, Newcastle, and Wales. It also created an eponymous national news website, and in 2021 it licensed its content to Facebook News (Table 5.9).

Table 5.9 JPIMedia

	Turnover (£m)	EBITDA (£m)	Margin %
2019	116.4	13.4	11.5
2020	88.2	7.7	8.7
2021	86.0	12.0	13.9

Source: Companies House filings

JPIMedia recouped its purchase price and more in its first full year of operation. A trading update issued in late 2021 announced that the company's transformation had been achieved more quickly than expected, and that it had £23 million cash in hand with which to make acquisitions (Tobitt, 2021, 16 December).

6   What If Newspapers Aren't Dying?

The *Independent*'s 2016 exit from print publication brought renewed predictions of the inevitable death of newspapers, but within a few years its surprising success online raised the possibility that digital news publications of quality could be economically viable. Newspaper fortunes rose as the decade drew to a close, only to be derailed by the COVID-19 pandemic in 2020. Increased consolidation suggested that if newspapers survived, they would be controlled by fewer owners. A moral panic over so-called fake news seen during the 2016 Brexit referendum and US presidential election campaigns brought a backlash against Facebook. Increasingly, publishers complained that it and Google were profiting from their news stories, links to which Facebook members shared and Google searches listed, alongside the first sentence or so of their content.

In 2016, a group of UK academics, union leaders, and politicians called on the government to impose a 1 percent levy on the digital giants to fund non-profit journalism. Google and Facebook were amassing 'eye-watering profits' while 'bleeding the newspaper industry dry by sucking up advertising revenue', they wrote in a letter to the *Guardian*. 'As national and local newspapers try to cut their way out of trouble by slashing editorial budgets and shedding staff, journalistic quality is becoming a casualty' (Stanistreet et al., 2016). In launching its Duopoly campaign in early 2017, *Press Gazette* pointed out that newspapers' share of the UK advertising market had declined in the previous decade from almost half to little more than 10 percent. 'We are seeking a fairer deal between news publishers and the digital giants – one which fairly rewards the creators of the content on which these platforms rely' (Ponsford, 2017, 10 April). Newsquest's CEO predicted later in 2017 that more newspapers would close unless the digital advertising market was regulated, telling the House of Lords communications committee that only a 'very few crumbs' were going to publishers (Linford, 2017, 30 November).

DOI: 10.4324/9780429469206-7

The 'fake news' scare gave publishers the upper hand in their fight with Google and Facebook, noted Buzzfeed, with media executives 'sensing blood in the water' (Perlberg & Di Stefano, 2017). The *Times* had engaged in a 'months-long campaign this year exposing various problems with tech platforms, particularly issues that have concerned advertisers', it added (Perlberg & Di Stefano, 2017). Murdoch had become an 'unlikely hero' to other media outlets in their war against Facebook and Google, according to Buzzfeed. 'Ultimately, sources close to Murdoch say that he hopes to push public opinion into viewing tech platforms more like Wall Street banks' (Perlberg & Di Stefano, 2017).

Events in early 2018 brought the narrative of newspaper peril to a crescendo, resulting in a series of inquiries. In February, the giant Trinity Mirror chain bought Northern & Shell for £127 million, adding its *Express* and *Star* daily and Sunday newspapers to its own *Mirror* titles and giving it eight national newspapers in addition to more than 110 local and regional titles. To reflect its increased scale, Trinity Mirror rebranded itself as Reach plc and, after closing its acquired *Star* weekly celebrity magazine, cut 70 staff and began to pool editorial resources at its seven remaining national titles to achieve £20 million in annual savings (Sweney, 2018, 12 September). The Competition and Markets Authority (CMA) investigated whether the acquisition would result in a substantial lessening of competition, while Ofcom looked into issues including plurality and editorial independence. Both cleared it, with Ofcom ruling that the merger may 'provide greater financial security to the combined group' and the CMA noting Reach's argument that structural changes in the industry 'threaten the long-term economic viability of smaller print publishers' (Tobitt, 2018, 20 June).

DCMS commissioned a report for the Cairncross Review which found that circulation and print advertising revenues of news publishers had dropped by more than half in the previous decade, from £6.8 billion in 2007 to £3.1 billion in 2017 (Mediatique, 2018). The report also found that the number of 'frontline' journalists had fallen from an estimated 23,000 to around 17,000 in the same period. It estimated that total editorial investment in print editorial content was £925 million in 2017, compared to £1.35 billion in 2011, a drop of 31 percent. From about 25 percent in 2007, the share of UK advertising expenditures going to print publications had plummeted to just 6 percent a decade later. Weekly circulation of local and regional newspapers fell by more than half in the same period, from 63.4 million to 31.4 million. Expenditure on national, local, and regional press advertising fell by a full £1 billion from 2012 to 2017. The report estimated that 136 local newspapers had shut down between 2012 and 2018, while 67 launched over the same period, 14 of which subsequently closed. 'The number of titles closed per year has increased, from 15 in 2012 to 45 in 2017' (Mediatique, 2018, p. 55).

> The majority of the titles that have closed since 2012 were freesheets, due to the weakness in advertising revenues and the greater competition from online media. Only two daily local newspapers closed between 2012 and 2018, while three launched . . . Of all the local newspapers that closed, 90 percent were in fact weekly newspapers.
>
> (Mediatique, 2018, p. 55)

The report noted that the average operating profit margin across the industry had gone down 'from 12 percent to zero' (Mediatique, 2018, p. 58). Johnston Press had gone from posting operating profit margins of about 30 percent in the early 2000s to margins in the teens, it added. Margins for national newspapers had been more variable, although their trendline was also broadly downward since the early 2000s. 'The key observation is that newspapers may find themselves in a vicious downward spiral' (Mediatique, 2018, p. 58). Newspapers faced numerous challenges in their quest to remain profitable, the report added, including the inability of most to make money online, and an increasing resistance by readers to paying ever higher cover prices. 'Circulation declines in the past could be to an extent offset by increases in cover prices. The ability to do so without losing paid-for readers seems to have dissipated' (Mediatique, 2018, p. 62). The report noted that a Local Journalism Partnership agreed between the BBC and the NMA in 2017 had funded 150 journalists with £8 million a year from the BBC licence fee to cover local authorities and public services. According to HoldTheFrontPage, however, most of the contracts have been won by the largest publishers Reach, Newsquest and Johnston Press. Scotland received the most so-called democracy reporters with 22, followed by the North West with 19 and Yorkshire and Lincolnshire with 16 (Linford, 2017, 7 December).

As the Cairncross Review was gathering evidence, however, Johnston Press finally lost its long race against its debt, which suggested to some that government inaction might soon have dire consequences for the nation's news media. Its profits in the first half of 2018 actually rose by more than half from the same period a year earlier to £6 million, however, buoyed by the performance of its acquired *i* newspaper, which had increased its circulation revenues by 17 percent and its advertising revenues by 20 percent (Linford, 2018). The problem for Johnston Press was the £220 million in debt which still hung around its neck like an anchor, and it had been unable to persuade its bondholders to grant it another refinancing. It slipped beneath the waves peacefully but not without protest that fall, having arranged a 'pre-packaged' bankruptcy to which its lenders and creditors agreed. The *Guardian*'s Roy Greenslade (2018) charged that Johnston Press had fallen prey to 'capitalism and greed'. Minority shareholders pointed out that the company was still profitable. Norwegian investor Christen Ager-Hanssen, who owned 20 percent, called its demise 'pre-planned corporate theft with all the parties colluding' (Pagano, 2018). The *Evening Standard* noted that the company's pension scheme, which had a deficit estimated at £109 million, did not transfer to its new owners but was instead assumed by the government's Pension Protection Fund. 'Magically, overnight, a new beast arose Phoenix-like from the ashes to take control of Johnston Press, in the guise of JPIMedia. But with the same bosses on board' (Pagano, 2018).

The new owner was US hedge fund GoldenTree Asset Management, which in 2010 had engineered a similar takeover of Canada's largest newspaper chain by buying up its distressed debt at deep discounts on the bond market. Hedge funds had taken over most of the major newspaper chains in North America since then, including seven of the ten largest in the United States and the two largest in Canada. They alone seemed to understand that there was still money to be made from newspapers, and more importantly that they still generated enough free cash flow to service a heavy debt load, which the hedge funds weaponised. In Canada, GoldenTree kept the bulk of its acquired debt on the books of the chain it renamed Postmedia Network, which owned most of the country's major dailies, not only ensuring that they were paid first every month but also necessitating deep cuts to its journalism as revenues fell (Edge, 2016).

Unbeknownst to most, newspaper publishers were making more money than they had in years. Companies House filings showed that by 2019 newspaper fortunes had improved considerably. *Daily Mail* publisher Associated Newspapers recorded a profit of £89.8 million that year and an EBITDA margin of 13.7 percent. Times Newspapers almost doubled its earnings in its 2019–20 fiscal year to £26.3 million, and in the pandemic year that followed they doubled again to £52.5 made at a profit margin of 16 percent. Reach saw its profits grow to £174.9 million in 2019 and its profit margin to 21.8 percent. Even the *Guardian*, which had lost tens of millions of pounds a year for almost a decade, had cut its losses to £3.7 million in 2019 on its way to making money in 2021, thanks to donations from readers (see Chapter 4). Profits in the provincial press were even more robust. Newsquest, which was by then owned by a US hedge fund, raised its profits to £38.3 million in 2019 and its margin to 20.3 percent. Reach Regionals Media Limited saw its earnings increase to £29.3 million in 2020 and its margin to 20.5 percent. Even JPIMedia, which was born out of bankruptcy in 2018 only because of the enormous debt which dragged Johnston Press down, made £13.4 million in 2019 at a profit margin of 11.5 percent (see Chapter 5).

The other development which gives hope to UK news media was the *Independent*'s ability to operate profitably as an online-only publication. Its digital arm had been profitable as a stand-alone unit even before the *Independent* exited print publication, but since then it has more than doubled its revenues, fully half of which came from outside the United Kingdom in 2020. Its earnings, expressed below as the company's reported operating profit, have been modest but its margin is comfortable, which suggests that it will remain a going concern.

Table 6.1 Independent Digital News & Media Ltd.

	Turnover (£m)	Profit (£m)	Margin %
2015	8.2	1.3	15.6
2016	14.2	1.7	12.0
2017	22.2	3.2	14.4
2018	24.8	3.0	12.1
2019	27.0	2.3	8.5
2020	30.2	2.7	8.9
2021	41.1	5.4	13.1

Year ending 30 September
Source: Companies House filings

The perception that newspapers were losing money and thus were doomed to extinction was based on the false assumption by many that falling circulation sales were an indicator of their fortunes. Instead, newspapers historically lost money with each copy sold only to make it all back and more from advertising. Publishers often kept their cover price low in order to increase sales and thus maximise ad revenues, or even gave their product away, as became widespread in the United Kingdom. With their advertising revenues falling, however, readers have been asked to pay more both for hard copies and for access to content online. The result has been nothing less than a reorganisation of the newspaper business model over the past decade or more. Pricing was always a chess game in the newspaper business, with two markets to serve – readers and advertisers – but with the advent of online publishing it became more like three-dimensional chess, with four revenue streams to maximise.

Contrary to perception, the business model for newspapers is hardly broken and in fact remains robust. Newspapers have nevertheless suffered great disruption from the Internet and are only now finding their way slowly to a sustainable future through experimentation, a process made more difficult by the ever-shifting media terrain. Few could have imagined as recently as the millennium that the market for digital advertising would soon be dominated by a search engine and a social network. Newspapers have adapted to a succession of new media in the past century – radio, television, and now the Internet – and they continue to find their niche, which admittedly grows narrower as attention choices expand (Table 6.1).

The shift to reader revenues has been complicated by several factors in the United Kingdom. A 2019 study found that a majority of the largest newspapers in other countries had adopted pay models, but not those in Italy or the United Kingdom, which were in 'very competitive markets where even leading titles may fear losing market share if they implement pay models' (Simon & Graves, 2019, p. 4). As the Cairncross report also noted:

> Unlike the U.S. and most of Europe, roughly 75 percent of sales of newspapers and magazines in the UK have been on newsstands. . . . UK publishers thus have almost no experience of accruing data on households to drive sales and service. Persuading their readers to pay by subscription is a new skill.
>
> (Cairncross, 2019, p. 48)

The problem at the local level, noted Lytollis (2021), is that readers have grown accustomed to getting their news for free, in either print or online. 'It's just a shame that people are being asked to pay for local news only after years of having it for free, and when publishers have slashed staff numbers, with a predictable impact on quality'. The introduction in 2017 of the Local Democracy Reporter Service funded by the BBC has alleviated that concern somewhat, however, and increasing it would arguably provide a more equitable alternative to forcing tech entrepreneurs to share their profits, especially if they do so voluntarily.

References

Anonymous. (2006, 26 August). Who killed the newspaper? *The Economist*, 9.

Anonymous. (2010, 10 June). The strange survival of ink. *The Economist*, 69.

Anonymous. (2018, 22 March). The Sun is toppled as Britain's biggest newspaper. *The Economist*. URL: www.economist.com/britain/2018/03/22/the-sun-is-toppled-as-britains-biggest-newspaper

Anonymous. (2020, 18 April). Breaking: News. *The Economist*, 20.

Anonymous. (2021, 14 December). The Guardian reaches one million digital subscriptions milestone. Guardian Online. URL: https://www.theguardian.com/gnm-press-office/2021/dec/14/the-guardian-reaches-one-million-digital-subscriptions-milestone

Armstrong, Ashley. (2016, 12 February). The Independent newspaper confirms an end to print production. *The Telegraph*. URL: www.telegraph.co.uk/finance/newsbysector/mediatechnologyandtelecoms/12153947/The-Independent-newspaper-confirms-an-end-to-print-production.html

Baistow, Tom. (1970). Anatomy of a crisis. In Boston, Richard, ed., *The Press We Deserve*. London: Routledge and Keegan Paul.

Bakker, Piet. (2013). The life cycle of a free newspaper business model in newspaper-rich markets. *Journalistica 1*, 33–51.

Barrès-Baker, M. C. (2006). An introduction to the early history of newspaper advertising. Brent Museum and Archive Occasional Publications, No. 2. URL: https://authorzilla.com/KNd5X/history-of-british-newspapers.html

Barrett, Steve. (2010, 23 September). Half my PR spend is wasted, and I know exactly which half. *PR Week*. URL: www.prweek.com/article/1266300/half-pr-spend-wasted-i-know-exactly-half

BBC. (2016, 6 January). Herald and Times Group announces further job losses. *BBC News*. URL: www.bbc.com/news/uk-scotland-scotland-business-35246860

Bintliff, Esther & Bradshaw, Tim. (2010, 16 July). Times' website visits fall by two-thirds. *Financial Times*. URL: www.ft.com/content/5a2bb6d6-910c-11df-b297-00144feab49a

Black, Conrad. (1993). *A Life in Progress*. Toronto: Key Porter.

Bloomgarden-Smoke, Kara (2014, 19 March). How "Journalism Crack" conquered the internet. *New York Observer*. URL: https://observer.com/2014/03/mailonline/

Bolger, Andrew. (2008, 3 December). Newspaper group axes 250 staff. *Financial Times*. URL: www.ft.com/content/9836604a-c190-11dd-831e-000077b07658

Bond, Shannon. (2018, 6 February). New York Times sees boom in online subscribers. *Financial Times*. URL: www.ft.com/content/bc312102-0cee-11e8-839d-41ca06376bf2

Boston, Richard, ed. (1970). *The Press We Deserve*. London: Routledge and Keegan Paul.

Boyce, George, Curran, James, & Wingate, Pauline, eds. (1978). *Newspaper History from the Seventeenth Century to the Present Day*. London: Constable.

Boyle, Darren. (2013, 28 December). Johnston Press announces deal to defer £300 million debt repayment. *Press Gazette*. URL: https://pressgazette.co.uk/johnston-press-announces-deal-to-defer-300-million-debt-repayment/

Braddon, Russell. (1968). *Roy Thomson of fleet street*. London: Fontana.

Brook, Stephen. (2009, 16 June). Half UK local and regional papers could shut by 2014, MPs are told. *Guardian Online*. URL: www.theguardian.com/media/2009/jun/16/half-local-papers-could-shut-2014

Bunz, Mercedes. (2010, 12 January). News International to block NewsNow from all its websites. *Guardian Online*. URL: www.theguardian.com/media/2010/jan/12/news-international-newsnow-sun-news-of-the-world

Burrell, Ian. (2009, 13 March). The big question: Why are regional papers in crisis, and does it matter if they close down? *The Independent*. URL: www.independent.co.uk/news/media/press/the-big-question-why-are-regional-papers-in-crisis-and-does-it-matter-if-they-close-down-1643916.html

Burrell, Ian. (2012, 24 April). Local newspapers: Read all about it? If only . . . *The Independent*. URL: www.independent.co.uk/news/media/press/local-newspapers-read-all-about-it-if-only-7670671.html

Cairncross, Frances. (2019). *The Cairncross Review: A Sustainable Future for Journalism*. URL: https://assets.publishing.service.gov.uk/government/uploads/system/uploads/attachment_data/file/779882/021919_DCMS_Cairncross_Review_.pdf

Cathcart, Brian. (2016, 11 February). The Independent ceasing to print would be the death of a medium, not of a message. *Guardian Online*. URL: www.theguardian.com/commentisfree/2016/feb/11/independent-ceasing-print-death-medium-not-message

Cawley, Anthony. (2017). Johnston Press and the crisis in Ireland's local newspaper industry, 2005–2014. *Journalism 18*(9), 1163–1183.

Chisolm, Jim. (2016). The next downturn: The launch pad for the new news. In Mair, John, Clark, Tor, Fowler, Neil, Snoddy, Raymond, & Tait, Richard, eds. *Last Words? How Can Journalism Survive the Decline of Print?* Suffolk, UK: Abramis Academic.

Chittum, Ryan. (2014, 19 February). Murdoch's hard-paywall success. *Columbia Journalism Review*. URL: https://archives.cjr.org/the_audit/murdochs_hard-paywall_success.php

Christopher, David. (2010, 8 March). Long Eaton, the town without a voice. *Press Gazette*. URL: https://pressgazette.co.uk/long-eaton-the-town-without-a-voice/

Clark, Tor. (2017). Missing the biggest story: The UK regional press after Leveson. *Journal of Applied Journalism and Media Studies 6*(1), 57–69.

Clarke, Bob. (2004). *From Grub Street to Fleet Street: An Illustrated History of English Newspapers to 1899*. Aldershot: Ashgate.

Connelly, Tony. (2015, 10 October). Newsquest reports profits of £70m while promising more cost cutting measures. *The Drum*. URL: www.thedrum.com/news/2015/10/10/newsquest-reports-profits-70m-while-promising-more-cost-cutting-measures

Connew, Paul. (2016). Don't switch off the life support . . . yet! In Mair, John, Clark, Tor, Fowler, Neil, Snoddy, Raymond, & Tait, Richard, eds. *Last Words? How Can Journalism Survive the Decline of Print?* Suffolk, UK: Abramis Academic.

Crisell, Andrew. (2003). *An Introductory History of British Broadcasting*. 2nd ed. London: Routledge.

Curran, James. (1978). The press as an agency of social control. In Boyce, George, Curran, James, & Wingate, Pauline, eds. *Newspaper History from the Seventeenth Century to the Present Day* (pp. 51–81). London: Constable.

Curran, James. (2003). *Power without Responsibility*. 6th ed. London: Routledge.

Davies, Nick & Hill, Amelia. (2011, 4 July). Missing Milly Dowler's voicemail was hacked by news of the world. *Guardian Online*. URL: www.theguardian.com/uk/2011/jul/04/milly-dowler-voicemail-hacked-news-of-world

De Lisle, Tim. (2014, 10 December). Can the Guardian survive? *The Economist*. URL: www.economist.com/1843/2014/12/10/can-the-guardian-survive

Edge, Marc. (2014). *Greatly Exaggerated: The Myth of the Death of Newspapers*. Vancouver: New Star Books.

Edge, Marc. (2016). *The News We Deserve: The Transformation of Canada's Media Landscape*. Vancouver: New Star Books.

Edge, Marc. (2020). Enabling Postmedia: Economists as the 'rock stars' of Canadian competition law. *Canadian Journal of Communication* 45(2), 287–303.

Evans, Harold. (2015). *Good Times, Bad Times: The Explosive Inside Story of Rupert Murdoch*. 5th ed. New York: Open Road Media.

Fenton, Ben. (2011, 24 June). Papers fight falling advertising. *Financial Times*. URL: www.ft.com/content/6974a162-1d58-11de-9eb3-00144feabdc0

Ferdinand, C. Y. (1997). *Benjamin Collins and the Provincial Newspaper Trade in the Eighteenth Century*. Oxford: Clarendon Press.

Fine, Jon. (2008, April 21). One newspaper that's in the pink. *BusinessWeek*, 77.

Finkelstein, David. (2020). *Edinburgh History of the British and Irish Press, Vol. 2: Expansion and Evolution, 1800–1900*. Edinburgh: Edinburgh University Press.

Flew, Terry. (2013, 7 August). Factcheck: Does Murdoch own 70% of newspapers in Australia? *The Conversation*. URL: https://theconversation.com/factcheck-does-murdoch-own-70-of-newspapers-in-australia-16812

Fowler, Neil. (2011, 10 November). *Have They Got News For You? The Rise, the Fall and the Future of Regional and Local Newspapers in the United Kingdom*. The Seventeenth Guardian Lecture delivered in Nuffield College, Oxford. URL: www.nuffield.ox.ac.uk/Resources/Guardian/Documents/Nuffield%20Guardian%20Lecture%202011.pdf

Franklin, Bob. (2006). *Local Journalism and Local Media: Making the Local News*. Abingdon: Routledge.

Franklin, Bob & Murphy, David. (1991). *What News? The Market, Politics and the Local Press*. London: Routledge.

Franklin, Bob & Murphy, David. (1998). *Making the Local News: Local Journalism in Context*. London: Routledge.

Galloway, Anthony. (2020, 10 October). Kevin Rudd creates petition for News Corp royal commission. *Sydney Morning Herald*. URL: www.smh.com.au/politics/federal/kevin-rudd-creates-petition-for-news-corp-royal-commission-20201010-p563vf.html

Gao, Pengjie, Lee, Chang, & Murphy, Dermot (2020). Financing dies in darkness? The impact of newspaper closures on public finance. *Journal of Financial Economics 135*(2), 445–467. URL: www.brookings.edu/wp-content/uploads/2018/04/Murphy-et-al.pdf

Gapper, John. (2009, 14 November). Murdoch will relish a battle over online pay walls. *Financial Times*, 9.

Gardner, Victoria E. M. (2016). *The Business of News in England, 1760–1820*. New York: Palgrave Macmillan.

Glover, Stephen. (2016, 18 March). Who guards the Guardian? *Prospect*. URL: www.prospectmagazine.co.uk/magazine/who-guards-the-guardian-2

Goldenberg, Susan. (1984). *The Thomson Empire*. Toronto: Methuen.

Goodfellow, Jessica. (2016, 5 August). The NUJ calls out "delusional" Johnston Press CEO after shares fall to an all-time low. *The Drum*. URL: www.thedrum.com/news/2016/08/05/nuj-calls-out-delusional-johnston-press-ceo-after-shares-fall-all-time-low

Granger, Jacob. (2019, 4 November). Future News Fund launches £2m pot for public service journalism following Cairncross Review. *Journalism.co.uk*. URL: www.journalism.co.uk/news/future-news-fund-launches-2m-public-service-journalism-pot-following-cairncross-recommendations/s2/a746914/

Granger, Jacob. (2020, 26 February). UK government will not fund public interest journalism, enlisting an IMPRESS-backed non-profit instead. *Journalism.co.uk*. URL: www.journalism.co.uk/news/public-interest-news-foundation-offers-support-for-journalism-outlets-following-cairncross-review/s2/a752270/

Greenslade, Roy. (2003). *Press Gang: How Newspapers Make Profits from Propaganda*. London: Macmillan.

Greenslade, Roy. (2011, 17 November). Johnston Press chief fails to spell out wonders of an online future. *Guardian Online*. URL: www.theguardian.com/media/greenslade/2011/nov/17/ashleyhighfield-johnston-press

Greenslade, Roy. (2013, 26 March). Telegraph to put up metered paywall. *Guardian Online*. URL: www.theguardian.com/media/greenslade/2013/mar/26/telegraph-paywall

Greenslade, Roy. (2014, 16 June). Claire Enders was wrong about newspaper closures, but she was also right. *Guardian Online*. URL: www.theguardian.com/media/greenslade/2014/jun/16/newspaper-closures-digital-media

Greenslade, Roy. (2015, 19 November). Newsquest fires veteran executives and orders them to quit the office. *Guardian Online*. URL: www.theguardian.com/media/greenslade/2015/nov/19/newsquest-fires-veteran-executives-and-orders-them-to-quit-the-office

Greenslade, Roy. (2015, 2 December). Now Boris Johnson must tackle Newsquest over lost jobs. *Guardian Online*. URL: www.theguardian.com/media/greenslade/2015/dec/02/now-boris-johnson-must-tackle-newsquest-over-lost-jobs

Greenslade, Roy. (2016, 14 September). What lies behind Trinity Mirror's return of four Metro franchises. *Guardian Online*. URL: www.theguardian.com/media/greenslade/2016/sep/14/metro

Greenslade, Roy. (2018, 14 October). Johnston Press falls prey to capitalism and greed. *Guardian Online*. URL: www.theguardian.com/media/commentisfree/2018/oct/14/johnston-press-finance-break-up-for-sale

Greenslade, Roy. (2020, 12 April). Why our newspapers might not survive the contagion of coronavirus. *Guardian Online*. URL: www.theguardian.com/media/commentisfree/2020/apr/12/newsprint-coronavirus-newspapers

Grueskin, Bill, Seave, Ava, & Graves, Lucas. (2011). *The Story So Far: What We Know about the Business of Digital Journalism*. New York: Columbia Journalism Review Books. URL: www.cjr.org/the_business_of_digital_journalism/the_story_so_far_what_we_know.php

Gulyas, Agnes. (2012). Changing business models and adaptation strategies of local newspapers. In Mair, John, Fowler, Neil, & Reeves, Ian eds. *What Do We Mean by Local? Grass Roots Journalism: Its Death and Rebirth*. St Edmunds: Abramis.

Habermas, Jurgen. (1991). *The Structural Transformation of the Public Sphere: An Inquiry into a Category of Bourgeois Society*. Cambridge: MIT Press.

Hall, Emma. (2009, 9 March). How Financial Times defies the times: Famed pink broadsheet in the black by raising price, charging for web. *Advertising Age*, 3.

Hancock, Matt. (2018, 1 March). *Oral Statement to Parliament: Leveson Consultation Response*. URL: www.gov.uk/government/speeches/leveson-consultation-response

Harker, Michael, Street, John, & Cross, Samuel. (2017). "Moving in concentric circles?" The history and politics of press inquiries. *Legal Studies 37*(2), 248–278.

Harris, Michael. (1978). The management of the London Newspaper Press during the eighteenth century. *Publishing History 4*, 95–112.

Hazlewood, Jack. (2016, 3 April). China spends big on propaganda in Britain . . . but returns are low. *Hong Kong Free Press*. URL: https://hongkongfp.com/2016/04/03/china-spends-big-on-propaganda-in-britain-but-returns-are-low/

Helm, Toby, Doward, Jamie, & Boffey, Daniel. (2011, 16 July). Rupert Murdoch's empire must be dismantled – Ed Miliband. *Guardian Online*. URL: www.theguardian.com/politics/2011/jul/16/rupert-murdoch-ed-miliband-phone-hacking

Henry, Jeff. (2016). Pop-up publishing: A new approach for print. In Mair, John, Clark, Tor, Fowler, Neil, Snoddy, Raymond, & Tait, Richard, eds. *Last Words? How Can Journalism Survive the Decline of Print?* Suffolk: Abramis Academic.

Herd, Harold. (1952). *The March of Journalism: The Story of the British Press from 1622 to the Present Day*. London: Allen & Unwin.

Hern, Alex. (2020, 27 November). Digital markets unit: What powers will new UK tech regulator have? *Guardian Online*. URL: www.theguardian.com/technology/2020/nov/27/digital-markets-unit-powers-new-uk-tech-regulator

Hill, John. (2016). *The British Newspaper Industry: The Future of the Regional Press*. New York: Palgrave Macmillan.

Hirsch, Fred & Gordon, David. (1975). *Newspaper Money: Fleet Street and the Search for the Affluent Reader*. London: Hutchinson.

Hirschorn, Michael. (2009, January/February). End times. *The Atlantic*. URL: www. theatlantic.com/magazine/archive/2009/01/end-times/307220/

Hobbs, Andrew. (2009). When the provincial press was the national press (c.1836– c.1900). *The International Journal of Regional and Local Studies 5*(1), 16–43.

Hobbs, Andrew. (2013). The deleterious dominance of *The Times* in nineteenth century historiography. *Journal of Victorian Culture 18*(4), 472–497.

Holahan, Catherine. (2007, August 10). The case for freeing the WSJ online. *Businessweek.com*. URL: www.businessweek.com/stories/2007-08-10/the-case-for-freeing-the-wsj-onlinebusinessweek-business-news-stock-market-and-financial-advice

Holmes, Tim, Hadwin, Sara, & Mottershed, Glyn. (2013). *The 21st Century Journalism Handbook: Essential Skills for the Modern Journalist*. London: Routledge.

House of Commons. (2010). Future for local and regional media. Culture, Media and Sport Committee, Fourth Report of Session, 2009–10, Vol. I. URL: https:// publications.parliament.uk/pa/cm200910/cmselect/cmcumeds/43/43i.pdf

House of Lords. (2020). Breaking news? The future of UK journalism. *Communications and Digital Committee*. URL: https://committees.parliament.uk/ publications/3707/documents/36111/default/

Howells, Rachel. (2015). Journey to the centre of a news black hole: Examining the democratic deficit in a town with no newspaper. PhD Thesis, Cardiff University.

Ives, Nat & Klaassen, Abbey. (2007, 13 August). Paid content on the net? Not if the content's news. *Advertising Age*, 3.

Jackson, Jasper. (2016, 27 July). Guardian's losses hit £69m but it gains more than 50,000 paying members. *Guardian Online*. URL: www.theguardian.com/ media/2016/jul/27/guardian-losses-members

Jackson, Jasper & Plunkett, John. (2015, 27 February). Financial Times to change way it charges for online content. *Guardian Online*. URL: www.theguardian. com/media/2015/feb/27/financial-times-to-change-way-it-charges-for-online-content

James, Meg. (2021, 17 February). Rupert Murdoch's news corp., Google reach deal on payments for journalism. *Los Angeles Times*. URL: www.latimes.com/ entertainment-arts/business/story/2021-02-17/rupert-murdoch-news-corp-google-deal-journalism

Jarvis, Jeff. (2009, 23 February). News sites should quit moaning about payment and just gopher it. *Guardian Online*. URL: www.theguardian.com/media/2009/ feb/23/digital-media-online-content

Jarvis, Jeff. (2010, 18 January). News Corp is foolish to block linking. *Guardian Online*. URL: www.theguardian.com/media/pda/2010/jan/18/news-corp-blocks-linking

Jarvis, Jeff. (2010, 26 March). Rupert Murdoch's pathetic paywall. *Guardian Online*. URL: www.theguardian.com/commentisfree/2010/mar/26/rupert-murdoch-pathetic-paywall

Jewell, John. (2013). How many drinks in that "last chance saloon"? The history of official inquiries into the British press. In Mair, John, ed. *After Leveson: The Future for British Journalism*. London: Arima.

Johnson, Branwell. (2004, 30 September). Advertisers feel the pull of the provinces. *Marketing Week*, 17–18.

Johnston, Chris. (2014, 14 November). Trinity Mirror to close seven local newspapers with the loss of 50 jobs. *Guardian Online*. URL: www.theguardian.com/media/2014/nov/14/trinity-mirror-close-local-newspapers-job-losees

Kaplan, David. (2009). Newser's Michael Wolff: In 18 months, 80% of newspapers will be gone: Give or take. *Forbes*. URL: www.forbes.com/2009/04/20/michael-wolff-newspapers-technology-paidcontent.html?sh=af8d7b64e803

Kersley, Andrew. (2022, 24 March). UK news media rich list: Top 50 highest-earning execs revealed. *Press Gazette*. URL: https://pressgazette.co.uk/highest-paying-jobs-media-uk-2022/

Kirsner, Scott. (1997, December). Profits in site? *American Journalism Review*. URL: https://ajrarchive.org/Article.asp?id=683

Kirwan, Peter. (2009, 10 August). I'm not an advocate, I'm a sceptic. *Guardian Online*. URL: www.theguardian.com/media/2009/aug/10/interview-claire-enders-analyis

Kitty, Alexandra. (2005). *Outfoxed: Rupert Murdoch's War on Journalism*. New York: Disinformation.

Krekhovetsky, Luba. (2003, 7 December). Sentiment is for losers. *Canadian Business 76*(23), 104–106.

Lavender, Tony, Wilkinson, Laura, Ramsay, Gordon, Stouli, Sami, Adshead, Stephen, & Chan, Yi Shen. (2020). *Research into Recent Dynamics of the Press Sector in the UK and Globally*. London: Plum Consulting. URL: https://assets.publishing.service.gov.uk/government/uploads/system/uploads/attachment_data/file/924325/Plum_DCMS_press_sector_dynamics_-_Final_Report_v4.pdf

Lee, Alan. J. (1976). *The Origins of the Popular Press in England, 1855–1914*. London: Croom Helm.

Lewin, Joel & Mance, Henry. (2015, 20 November). Johnston Press shares fall to all-time low as print ad sales shrink. *Financial Times*, 21.

Lewis, Justin, Williams, Andrew, & Franklin, Bob. (2008). A compromised fourth estate? UK news journalism, public relations and news sources. *Journalism Studies 9*(1), 1–20.

Linford, Paul. (2014, 16 June). Editor's blog: Why Claire Enders was wrong about newspaper closures. *HoldtheFrontPage*. URL: www.holdthefrontpage.co.uk/2014/news/editors-blog-why-claire-enders-was-wrong-about-newspaper-closures/

Linford, Paul. (2017, 30 November). More titles will close unless ad market is regulated, says Newsquest boss. *HoldtheFrontPage*. URL: www.holdthefrontpage.co.uk/2017/news/more-titles-will-close-unless-ad-market-is-regulated-says-newsquest-boss/

Linford, Paul. (2017, 7 December). Big groups win lion's share of BBC local reporting contracts. *HoldtheFrontPage*. URL: www.holdthefrontpage.co.uk/2017/news/ldr-contracts/

Linford, Paul. (2018, 29 August). Market for regional titles extremely difficult says JP despite profit rise. *HoldtheFrontPage*. URL: www.holdthefrontpage.co.uk/2018/news/market-for-regional-titles-extremely-difficult-says-jp-despite-profit-rise/

Linford, Paul. (2020, 6 April). Reach plc to furlough a fifth of all staff and cut pay by 10pc. *HoldtheFrontPage*. URL: www.holdthefrontpage.co.uk/2020/news/reach-plc-to-furlough-a-fifth-of-all-staff-and-cut-pay-by-10pc/

Luft, Oliver. (2009, 12 November). Weekly Birmingham Post launched. *Press Gazette*. URL: https://pressgazette.co.uk/weekly-birmingham-post-launched/

Lytollis, Roger. (2021, 5 August). Giving away news online didn't pay and led to print slump, says ex-local journalist behind new memoir. *Press Gazette*. URL: https://pressgazette.co.uk/giving-away-news-online-didnt-pay-and-led-to-print-slump-says-ex-local-journalist/

MacMillan, Arthur (2012). The sad decline of The Scotsman. *British Journalism Review 23*(4), 64–69. URL: www.bjr.org.uk/archive+the_sad_decline_of_the_scotsman

Mance, Henry. (2016). National media groups re-evaluate their business model and ways to promote content. *Financial Times*. URL: www.ft.com/content/0aa8beac-c44f-11e5-808f-8231cd71622e

Martin, Jonathan & Burns, Alexander. (2022). *This Will Not Pass: Trump, Biden, and the Battle for America's Future*. New York: Simon & Schuster.

Martinson, Jane. (2016, 25 January). Guardian News & Media to cut costs by 20%. *Guardian Online*. URL: www.theguardian.com/media/2016/jan/25/guardian-news-media-to-cut-running-costs

Martinson, Jane. (2016, 17 March). Guardian Media Group to cut 250 jobs in bid to break even within three years. *Guardian Online*. URL: www.theguardian.com/media/2016/mar/17/guardian-media-group-to-cut-250-jobs

Matthews, Rachel. (2015). The provincial press in England: An overview. In Conboy, Martin & Steel, John, eds. *The Routledge Companion to British Media History* (pp. 239–249). Oxford: Routledge.

Matthews, Rachel. (2017). *The History of the Provincial Press in England*. London: Bloomsbury Academic.

Mayhew, Freddy. (2020, 7 April). News publishers hit new online records with coronavirus coverage. *Press Gazette*. URL: https://pressgazette.co.uk/ft-and-reach-titles-hit-new-online-records-with-coronavirus-coverage/

Mayhew, Freddy. (2021, 21 October). Financial Times files £34.5m loss in UK for 2020, but states "small" profit globally. *Press Gazette*. URL: https://pressgazette.co.uk/financial-times-files-34-5m-loss-in-uk-for-2020-but-states-small-profit-globally/

McCord, Richard. (2001). *The Chain Gang: One Newspaper Versus the Gannett Empire*. Columbia, USA: University of Missouri Press.

McIntyre, Douglas A. (2009, 9 March). The 10 most endangered newspapers in America. *Time.com*. URL: http://content.time.com/time/business/article/0,8599,1883785,00.html

McLuhan, Marshall. (1964). *Understanding Media: The Extensions of Man*. London: Routledge & Kegan Paul.

McNally, Paul. (2008, 12 December). Enders: Urgent action needed to save newspapers. *Press Gazette*. URL: https://pressgazette.co.uk/enders-urgent-action-needed-to-save-newspapers/

Meade, Amanda. (2021, 9 December). "Dangerous monopoly": Labor and Greens support judicial inquiry into media diversity and News Corp. *Guardian Online*.

URL: www.theguardian.com/media/2021/dec/09/dangerous-monopoly-labor-and-greens-support-judicial-inquiry-into-media-diversity-and-news-corp

Media Reform Coalition. (2014). *The Elephant in the Room: A Survey of Media Ownership and Plurality in the United Kingdom.* URL: www.mediareform.org.uk/wp-content/uploads/2014/04/ElephantintheroomFinalfinal.pdf

Media Reform Coalition. (2015). *Who Owns the UK Media?* London: University of London. URL: www.mediareform.org.uk/wp-content/uploads/2015/10/Who_owns_the_UK_media-report_plus_appendix1.pdf

Media Reform Coalition. (2019). *Who Owns the UK Media?* London: University of London. URL: www.mediareform.org.uk/wp-content/uploads/2019/03/Who_Owns_the_UK_Media_2019.pdf

Media Reform Coalition. (2021). *Who Owns the UK Media?* London: University of London. URL: www.mediareform.org.uk/wp-content/uploads/2021/03/Who-Owns-the-UK-Media_final2.pdf

Media Reform Coalition. (2022, 8 March). *Newsquest's Acquisition of Archant: More Bad News for Local Journalism.* URL: www.mediareform.org.uk/blog/newsquests-acquisition-of-archant-more-bad-news-for-local-journalism

Mediatique. (2018). *Overview of Recent Dynamics in the UK Press Market.* London: Mediatique Limited. URL: https://assets.publishing.service.gov.uk/government/uploads/system/uploads/attachment_data/file/778155/180621_Mediatique_-_Overview_of_recent_dynamics_in_the_UK_press_market_-_Report_for_DCMS.pdf

Membery, York. (2010). Who killed the News Chronicle? *British Journalism Review* *21*(1), 66–72.

Meyer, Philip. (2004). *The Vanishing Newspaper: Saving Journalism in the Information Age.* Columbia, USA: University of Missouri Press.

Monopolies Commission. (1966). *The Times Newspaper and the Sunday Times Newspaper: A Report on the Proposed Transfer to a Newspaper Proprietor.* London: Her Majesty's Stationery Office.

Moss, Stephen. (2009, 3 April, p. 4). Across the country, local newspapers are being cut to the bone or closed down. Is regional journalism doomed? And if it is, what does that mean for local democracy? *The Guardian.*

Murdock, Graham & Golding, Peter. (1978). The structure, ownership and control of the press, 1914–76. In Boyce, George, Curran, James, & Wingate, Pauline, eds. *Newspaper History from the Seventeenth Century to the Present Day.* London: Constable.

Mutter, Alan. (2009, 8 February). Mission possible? Charging for web content. *Reflections of a Newsosaur.* URL: http://newsosaur.blogspot.com/2009/02/mission-possible-charging-for-content.html

Negrine, Ralph. (1994). *Politics and the Mass Media in Britain.* 2nd ed. London: Routledge.

Negrine, Ralph M., ed. (1999). *Television and the Press Since 1945.* Manchester: Manchester University Press.

Nel, Francois. (2010). *Laid Off: What do UK journalists do next?* Preston: University of Central Lancashire. URL: https://www.journalism.co.uk/uploads/laidoffreport.pdf

Nel, Francois. (2013). *Pressed to Change: Business Model Innovation and Integration in the British Local Newspaper Industry*. Preston: University of Central Lancashire.

Newman, Nic. (2022). Journalism, media, and technology trends and predictions. *Reuters Institute for the Study of Journalism*. URL: https://reutersinstitute.politics.ox.ac.uk/sites/default/files/2022-01/Newman%20-%20Trends%20and%20Predictions%202022%20FINAL.pdf

News Corp. (2021). *Application to the Secretary of State*. URL: https://assets.publishing.service.gov.uk/government/uploads/system/uploads/attachment_data/file/995665/Annex_B_-_Redacted_-_DCMS_Application.pdf

Nilsson, Patricia. (2021, 13 August). Local newsrooms still holding the front page for recovery. *Financial Times*. URL: www.ft.com/content/28bfe0c1-d17f-4cde-8c23-8166628e1aad

Oborne, Peter. (2015, 17 February). Why I have resigned from the Telegraph. *openDemocracy*. URL: www.opendemocracy.net/en/opendemocracyuk/why-i-have-resigned-from-telegraph/

Ofcom. (2018, 23 November). *The Operation of the Media Ownership Rules Listed under Section 391 of the Communications Act 2003*. URL: www.ofcom.org.uk/__data/assets/pdf_file/0030/127929/Media-ownership-rules-report-2018.pdf

Ofcom. (2021, 17 November). *The Future of Media Plurality in the UK*. URL: www.ofcom.org.uk/__data/assets/pdf_file/0019/228124/statement-future-of-media-plurality.pdf

Ogbebor, Binakuromo. (2020). *British Media Coverage of the Press Reform Debate: Journalists Reporting Journalism*. London: Palgrave Macmillan.

Oliver & Ohlbaum Associates. (2015). *The News Market in the 21st Century and the Likely Implications for the BBC's Role*. London: News Media Association. URL: www.newsmediauk.org/write/MediaUploads/PDF%20Docs/OandO_NMA_-_UK_news_provision_at_the_crossroads.pdf

O'Malley, Tom. (2014). The regulation of the press. In Conboy, M. & Steel, J., eds. *The Routledge Companion to British Media History*. London: Routledge.

O'Reilly, Lara & Edwards, Jim. (2014, 16 December). These are the UK newspapers failing to tackle the switch to digital. *Business Insider*. URL: http://uk.businessinsider.com/the-state-of-the-uk-national-newspaper-industry-2014-12?r=US

Osborne Clarke. (2016, 22 February). Telegraph Media Group defend native advertising. *Osborne Clarke.com*. URL: https://marketinglaw.osborneclarke.com/marketing-techniques/now-michelin-and-telegraph-media-group-defend-native-advertising/

Pagano, Margareta. (2018, 22 November). Johnston's pension dump highlights pre-pack perils. *Evening Standard*. URL: www.standard.co.uk/business/johnston-s-pension-dump-highlights-prepack-perils-a3997116.html

Palser, Barb. (2008, February/March). Free at last. *American Journalism Review*. URL: https://ajrarchive.org/Article.asp?id=4471

Perch, Keith. (2016). The collapse of the business model of regional newspapers has been far greater than previously stated and is undermining public sphere journalism. In Mair, John, Clark, Tor, Fowler, Neil, Snoddy, Raymond, & Tait, Richard, eds. *Last Words? How Can Journalism Survive the Decline of Print?* Bury St Edmunds, UK: Abramis.

Perlberg, Steven & Di Stefano, Mark. (2017, 4 October). Rupert Murdoch is the media's unlikely hero in the war against Facebook and Google. *Buzzfeed*. URL: www.buzzfeednews.com/article/stevenperlberg/rupert-murdoch-is-the-medias-unlikely-hero-against-tech

Political and Economic Planning. (1938). *Report on the British Press: A Survey of Its Current Operations and Problems with Special Reference to National Newspapers and Their Part in Public Affairs*. London: PEP.

Ponsford, Dominic. (2012, 26 April). Johnson [sic.] press: Zombie company? *New Statesman*. URL: www.newstatesman.com/politics/2012/04/johnson-press-zombie-company

Ponsford, Dominic. (2012, 28 November). Revealed: Regional press group's plan to hide £51.3m in profits from staff and competitors. *Press Gazette*. URL: https://pressgazette.co.uk/revealed-regional-press-groups-plan-to-hide-513m-in-profits-from-staff-and-competitors/

Ponsford, Dominic. (2015, 27 August). The survival of UK regional dailies and their digital growth is the great escape story of the media downturn. *Press Gazette*. URL: www.pressgazette.co.uk/the-survival-of-uk-regional-dailies-and-their-digital-growth-is-the-great-escape-story-of-the-media-downturn

Ponsford, Dominic. (2016, 9 November). Dundee daily follows Aberdeen sister title and puts online content behind metered paywall. *Press Gazette*. URL: https://pressgazette.co.uk/dundee-daily-follows-aberdeen-sister-title-and-puts-online-content-behind-metered-paywall/

Ponsford, Dominic. (2017, 17 March). Guardian could be making more than £25m from members and digital subscribers, but ad income down £11m this year. *Press Gazette*. URL: https://pressgazette.co.uk/who-says-millennials-dont-read-newspapers-editor-ted-young-on-the-rise-and-rise-of-metro/

Ponsford, Dominic. (2017, 24 March). Who says millennials don't read newspapers? *Press Gazette*. URL: https://pressgazette.co.uk/who-says-millennials-dont-read-newspapers-editor-ted-young-on-the-rise-and-rise-of-metro/

Ponsford, Dominic. (2017, 10 April). Press Gazette launches Duopoly campaign to stop Google and Facebook destroying journalism. *Press Gazette*. URL: www.pressgazette.co.uk/press-gazette-launches-duopoly-campaign-to-stop-google-and-facebook-destroying-journalism/

Ponsford, Dominic. (2017, 21 November). Financial Times surpasses 700,000 digital subscribers and boasts highest readership in 130-year history. *Press Gazette*. URL: www.pressgazette.co.uk/financial-times-surpasses-700000-digital-subscribers-and-boasts-highest-readership-in-130-year-history/

Press Gazette. (2007, 14 May). Hiding the heartbreak behind the regional revenue decline. *Press Gazette*. URL: https://pressgazette.co.uk/hiding-the-heartbreak-behind-the-regional-revenue-decline/

Press Gazette. (2014, 4 March). Guardian "secure for generations to come" after tax-free bonanza of £619m from Auto Trader sale. *Press Gazette*. URL: www.pressgazette.co.uk/guardian-secure-for-generations-to-come-after-tax-free-bonanza-of-619m-from-auto-trader-sale/

Preston, Peter. (2016). I have seen the print future . . . . Does it work? In Mair, John, Clark, Tor, Fowler, Neil, Snoddy, Raymond, & Tait, Richard, eds. *Last*

Words? How Can Journalism Survive the Decline of Print? Suffolk, UK: Abramis Academic.

Preston, Peter. (2016, 11 September). Gannett hovers over Richmond. *Guardian Online*. URL: www.theguardian.com/media/2016/sep/11/gannett-hovers-richmond-newsquest-dimblebys

Ramsay, Gordon & Moore, Martin. (2016). *Monopolising Local News: Is There an Emerging Local Democratic Deficit in the UK Due to the Decline of Local Newspapers?* The Policy Institute at King's College London. URL: www.kcl.ac.uk/policy-institute/assets/cmcp/local-news.pdf

Rayner, Gordon. (2011, 18 June). Riches to rags as Guardian bleeds £33m in a year. *The Telegraph*. URL: www.telegraph.co.uk/finance/newsbysector/mediatechnologyandtelecoms/media/8583220/Riches-to-rags-as-Guardian-bleeds-33m-in-a-year.html

Reach plc. (2022). *Annual Report*. URL: www.reachplc.com/content/dam/reach/corporate/documents/results-and-reports/Reach_AnnualReport2021.pdf.downloadasset.pdf

Research and Markets. (2014). Newspapers market report 2014. *Manufacturing Close-Up*. URL: www.researchandmarkets.com/research/g7d4gz/newspapers_market

Rigby, Elizabeth. (2015, 26 November). Online but off the pace as Mail website misses target. *The Times*. URL: www.thetimes.co.uk/article/online-but-off-the-pace-as-mail-website-misses-target-mb9zhswmjkg

Royal Commission on the Press (RCTP) 1947–49. (1949). *Report*. London: His Majesty's Stationery Office.

Royal Commission on the Press (RCTP) 1961–62. (1962a). *Documentary Evidence Vol. Ii: Provincial Daily and Sunday Newspaper Undertakings in England: Daily and Sunday Newspaper Undertakings in Scotland, Wales and Northern Ireland.* London: Her Majesty's Stationery Office.

Royal Commission on the Press (RCTP) 1961–62. (1962b). *Report*. London: Her Majesty's Stationery Office.

Royal Commission on the Press (RCTP) 1974–77. (1976). *Interim Report: The National Newspaper Industry*. London: Her Majesty's Stationery Office.

Royal Commission on the Press. (RCTP) 1974–77. (1977a). *Final Report*. London: Her Majesty's Stationery Office.

Royal Commission on the Press. (RCTP) 1974–77. (1977b). *Concentration of Ownership in the Provincial Press*. London: Her Majesty's Stationery Office.

Rusbridger, Alan. (2018). *Breaking News: The Remaking of Journalism and Why It Matters Now*. Edinburgh: Canongate.

Sabbagh, Dan & Halliday, Josh. (2012, 1 May). Rupert Murdoch deemed "not a fit person" to run international company. *Guardian Online*. URL: www.theguardian.com/media/2012/may/01/rupert-murdoch-not-fit-phone-hacking

Schlesinger, Philip & Doyle, Gillian. (2014). From organizational crisis to multi-platform salvation? Creative destruction and the recomposition of news media. *Journalism 16*(3), 305–323.

Schulhofer-Wohl, Sam & Garrido, Miguel. (2009). Do newspapers matter? Short-run and long-run evidence from the closure of The Cincinnati Post.

Working Paper No. 14817, National Bureau of Economic Research, Cambridge, MA, USA. URL: www.nber.org/system/files/working_papers/w14817/w14817.pdf

Shaker, Lee. (2014). Dead newspapers and citizens' civic engagement. *Political Communication 31*(1), 131–148.

Sharman, David. (2020, 3 April). Around 150 journalists across local press now on paid leave as Archant joins furlough scheme. *HoldtheFrontPage*. URL: www.holdthefrontpage.co.uk/2020/news/regional-publisher-to-furlough-small-number-of-staff/

Sharman, David. (2020, 15 April). Newspaper launches donation drive as half of staff furloughed. *HoldtheFrontPage*. URL: www.holdthefrontpage.co.uk/2020/news/newspaper-launches-donation-drive-as-half-of-staff-furloughed/

Sharman, David. (2020, 7 July). Reach to axe 550 jobs after coronavirus hits business. *HoldtheFrontPage*. URL: www.holdthefrontpage.co.uk/2020/news/reach-to-axe-550-jobs-after-coronavirus-hits-business/

Sharman, David. (2021, 6 January). Impact of coronavirus "not as pronounced as anticipated" says publisher. *HoldtheFrontPage*. URL: www.holdthefrontpage.co.uk/2021/news/publisher-says-impact-of-coronavirus-not-as-pronounced-as-anticipated/

Sharman, David. (2021, 8 January). Reach reveals expected £135m profit after record digital performance. *HoldtheFrontPage*. URL: www.holdthefrontpage.co.uk/2021/news/reach-reveals-expected-135m-profit-after-record-digital-performance/

Sharman, David. (2021, 28 October). Number of young people reading local news up by one-fifth, figures show. *HoldtheFrontPage*. URL: www.holdthefrontpage.co.uk/2021/news/number-of-young-people-reading-local-news-up-by-one-fifth-figures-show/

Sharman, David. (2021, 7 December). Journalism jobs boom hailed as ex-editor says past cuts went "too far". *HoldtheFrontPage*. URL: www.holdthefrontpage.co.uk/2021/news/journalism-jobs-boom-hailed-as-ex-editor-says-past-cuts-went-too-far/

Shirky, Clay. (2009, 13 March). Newspapers and thinking the unthinkable. *Shirky. com*. URL: www.shirky.com/weblog/2009/03/newspapers-and-thinking-the-unthinkable/

Siklos, Richard. (1996). *Shades of Black: Conrad Black and the World's Fastest Growing Press Empire*. Toronto: McClelland & Stewart.

Silberstein-Loeb, Jonathan. (2009). The structure of the news market in Britain, 1870–1914. *Business History Review 83*(4), 759–788.

Simon, Felix M. & Graves, Lucas. (2019, May). Pay models for online news in the US and Europe: 2019 update. *Reuters Institute for the Study of Journalism*. URL: https://reutersinstitute.politics.ox.ac.uk/sites/default/files/2019-05/Paymodels_for_Online_News_FINAL_1.pdf

Simons, Margaret. (2020, 16 October). "Culture of fear": Why Kevin Rudd is determined to see an end to Murdoch's media dominance. *Guardian Online*. URL: www.theguardian.com/media/2020/oct/17/culture-of-fear-why-kevin-rudd-is-determined-to-see-an-end-to-murdochs-media-dominance

Simpson, John. (2010). *Unreliable Sources: How the 20th Century Was Reported*. London: Macmillan.

Slauter, Will. (2015). The rise of the newspaper. In John, Richard R. & Silberstein-Loeb, Jonathan, eds. *Making News: The Political Economy of Journalism in Britain and America from the Glorious Revolution to the Internet*. Oxford: Oxford University Press.

Smith, A. C. H. (1970). Provincial press: Towards one big shopper. In Boston, Richard, ed. *The Press We Deserve*. London: Routledge and Keegan Paul.

Snoddy, Raymond. (1992). *The Good, the Bad, and the Unacceptable: The Hard News about the British Press*. London: Faber and Faber.

Southern, Lucinda. (2018, 11 July). How the Telegraph ties native ads to brand metrics. *Digiday*. URL: https://digiday.com/media/telegraph-ties-native-ads-brand-metrics/

Spencer, David R. (2007). *The Yellow Journalism and the Rise of America as a World Power*. Evanston, USA: Northwestern University Press.

Stanistreet, Michelle and 27 others. (2016, 11 November). Support new news providers via a levy on digital giants like Google and Facebook [letter to the editor]. *Guardian Online*. URL: www.theguardian.com/media/2016/nov/11/protect-newspapers-via-a-levy-on-digital-giants-like-google-and-facebook

Steinbock, Dan. (2000). Building dynamic capabilities: The wall street journal interactive edition: A successful online subscription model (1993–2000). *International Journal on Media Management 2*(3/4), 178–194.

Stephens, Donna Lampkin. (2015). *If It Ain't Broke, Break It: How Corporate Journalism Killed the Arkansas Gazette*. Fayetteville, USA: University of Arkansas Press.

Stephens, Mitchell. (1997). *A History of News*. New York: Harcourt Brace.

Sweney, Mark. (2014, 22 January). Independent website could net Lebedevs millions in standalone sale. *Guardian Online*. URL: www.theguardian.com/media/2014/jan/22/independent-website-lebedevs-standalone-sale

Sweney, Mark. (2015, 19 November). Newsquest boosts profits while cutting more than 220 staff. *Guardian Online*. URL: www.theguardian.com/media/2015/oct/09/newsquest-boosts-profits-while-cutting-more-than-220-staff

Sweney, Mark. (2016, 9 May). Express triples profits by cutting jobs and print costs as turnover drop. *Guardian Online*. URL: www.theguardian.com/media/2016/may/09/express-newspapers-richard-desmond-pre-tax-profits

Sweney, Mark. (2016, 3 November). Telegraph axes metered paywall and launches premium subscription service. *Guardian Online*. URL: www.theguardian.com/media/2016/nov/03/telegraph-paywall-premium-subscriptions

Sweney, Mark. (2018, 12 September). Publisher of Mirror and Express newspapers to cut 70 jobs. *Guardian Online*. URL: www.theguardian.com/business/2018/sep/12/publisher-of-mirror-and-express-newspapers-to-cut-70-jobs-reach

Sweney, Mark. (2018, 3 October). Telegraph to put politics, business and rugby news behind paywall. *Guardian Online*. URL: www.theguardian.com/media/2018/oct/03/telegraph-to-put-politics-business-and-rugby-news-behind-paywall

Temple, Michael. (2008). *The British Press*. Maidenhead: McGraw-Hill Education.

Temple, Michael. (2017). *The Rise and Fall of the British Press*. London: Routledge.

Thorpe, Vanessa & Meade, Amanda. (2020, 22 November). Ex-PMs unite in Australia in bid to curb power of Murdoch empire. *Guardian Online*. URL:

www.theguardian.com/media/2020/nov/22/ex-pms-unite-in-australia-in-bid-to-curb-power-of-murdoch-empire

Thurman, Neil & Fletcher, Richard. (2018). Are newspapers heading toward post-print obscurity? A case study of the Independent's transition to online-only. *Digital Journalism 6*(8), 1003–17.

Tobitt, Charlotte. (2018, 20 June). Culture Secretary gives green light to Reach takeover of Express Newspapers. *Press Gazette*. URL: https://pressgazette.co.uk/culture-secretary-gives-green-light-to-reach-takeover-of-express-newspapers/

Tobitt, Charlotte. (2018, 25 September). IPSO, NUJ, NMA and Johnston Press editors call on Cairncross Review to make tech giants "give something back" to publishers but Impress fears missing "the bigger picture". *Press Gazette*. URL: https://pressgazette.co.uk/ipso-nuj-and-johnston-press-editors-call-on-cairncross-review-to-make-tech-giants-give-something-back-to-publishers-but-impress-fears-missing-the-bigger-picture/

Tobitt, Charlotte. (2021, 27 January). DC Thomson launches recruitment drive for about 20 jobs in online "future proof" plan. *Press Gazette*. URL: https://pressgazette.co.uk/dc-thomson-launches-recruitment-20-jobs-online-future-proof-plan/

Tobitt, Charlotte. (2021, 19 April). Reach settles with staff who lodged claim over 10% Covid pay cut. *Press Gazette*. URL: https://pressgazette.co.uk/reach-settles-staff-who-lodged-claim-10-covid-pay-cut/

Tobitt, Charlotte. (2021, 27 July). Reach says it will employ more journalists than at any point in past decade by end of 2021. *Press Gazette*. URL: https://pressgazette.co.uk/reach-says-it-will-employ-more-journalists-than-at-any-point-in-last-decade-by-end-of-2021/

Tobitt, Charlotte. (2021, 10 August). Archant, Newsquest and MNA halve furlough claims as support scheme winds down. *Press Gazette*. URL: https://pressgazette.co.uk/archant-newsquest-mna-halve-news-media-furlough-claims-may-2021/

Tobitt, Charlotte. (2021, 3 November). Lord Rothermere agrees £3bn deal to take Mail, Metro and i publisher DMGT private. *Press Gazette*. URL: www.pressgazette.co.uk/dmgt-private-lord-rothermere/

Tobitt, Charlotte. (2021, 16 December). David Montgomery's National World eyes cost cuts and acquisitions in 2022. *Press Gazette*. URL: https://pressgazette.co.uk/david-montgomerys-national-world-eyes-cost-cuts-and-acquisitions-in-2022/

Tobitt, Charlotte. (2022, 10 February). Nadine Dorries ends restrictions on Times/Sunday Times editorial independence. *Press Gazette*. URL: https://pressgazette.co.uk/times-sunday-times-restrictions-editorial-independence/

Tracy, Marc. (2021, 4 February). The New York Times tops 7.5 million subscriptions as ads decline. *New York Times*. URL: www.nytimes.com/2021/02/04/business/media/new-york-times-earnings.html

Tryhorn, Chris. (2005, 2 February). Murdoch: Metro has hit the Sun. *Guardian Online*. URL: www.theguardian.com/media/2005/feb/02/rupertmurdoch.pressandpublishing

Turvill, William. (2014, 27 May). DC Thomson's Press and Journal launches website behind metered paywall. *Press Gazette*. URL: https://pressgazette.co.uk/dc-thomsons-press-and-journal-launches-website-behind-metered-paywall/

Turvill, William. (2015, 8 October). Johnston Press closures mean more than 300 UK local newspapers have gone in last ten years. *Press Gazette*. URL: www. pressgazette.co.uk/johnston-press-closures-mean-more-300-uk-local-newspapers-have-been-closed-ten-years/

Turvill, William. (2021, 28 October). Covid comeback: News Corp, NYT, Gannett, DMGT, reach and future market caps surpass pre-pandemic heights. *Press Gazette*. URL: https://pressgazette.co.uk/media-company-share-prices/

Turvill, William & Ponsford, Dominic. (2015, 19 February). *Commercial Influence over Editorial Has Been "Telegraph's Dirty Little Secret for Some Time" Says Former Staffer*. URL: https://pressgazette.co.uk/peter-oborne-spot-say-sources-commercial-power-over-editorial-has-been-telegraphs-dirty-little/

van Duyn, Aline & Waters Richard. (2006, 7 August). Google in $900m ad deal with MySpace. *Financial Times*. URL: www.ft.com/content/17e8e67e-2660-11db-afa1-0000779e2340

Walker, R. B. (1973): Advertising in London Newspapers, 1650–1750. *Business History 15*(2), 112–130.

Waterson, Jim. (2018, 25 September). UK newspaper industry demands levy on tech firms. *Guardian Online*. URL: www.theguardian.com/media/2018/sep/25/uk-newspaper-industry-demands-levy-on-tech-firms

Weiss, Philip. (1987, 2 February). The invasion of the Gannettoids. *New Republic 196*(5), 18–22.

Wiener, Joel. H. (2014). The nineteenth century and the emergence of a mass circulation press. In Conboy, Martin & Steel, John, eds. *The Routledge Companion to British Media History*. London: Routledge.

Williams, Andy. (2010, 17 July). Unholy Trinity: The decline of Welsh news media. *openDemocracy*. URL: www.opendemocracy.net/en/opendemocracyuk/unholy-trinity-decline-of-welsh-news-media/

Williams, Andy. (2011). Stop press? The crisis in Welsh newspapers, and what to do about it. *Cyfrwng: Media Wales Journal 10*, 71–80.

Williams, Andy. (2017, 23 May). 7 shocking local news industry trends which should terrify you. National *Assembly for Wales, Culture, Welsh Language and Communications Committee, News Journalism in Wales, Evidence*. URL: https://business.senedd.wales/documents/s63454/NJW10%20Dr.%20Andy%20Williams%20Cardiff%20University%20-%20Local%20News.pdf

Williams, Andy & Franklin, Bob. (2007). *Turning around the Tanker: Implementing Trinity Mirror's Online Strategy*. Cardiff: Cardiff University. URL: http://image.guardian.co.uk/sys-files/Media/documents/2007/03/13/Cardiff.Trinity.pdf

Williams, Christopher. (2016, 30 September). Daily Mail owner cuts 400 jobs in top-to-bottom review. *Daily Telegraph*, 3.

Williams, Francis. (1957). *Dangerous Estate*. New York: Longmans.

Williams, Kevin. (2010). *Read All about It: A History of the British Newspaper*. Abingdon: Routledge.

Wills, Doug. (2016). The right time, the right place, and a changed business model. In Mair, John, Clark, Tor, Fowler, Neil, Snoddy, Raymond, & Tait, Richard, eds. *Last Words? How Can Journalism Survive the Decline of Print?* Suffolk, UK: Abramis Academic.

Wright, Oliver & Grice, Andrew. (2011, 14 July). News International broke law on huge scale, says ex-PM. *The Independent*. URL: www.independent.co.uk/news/media/press/news-international-broke-law-on-huge-scale-says-expm-2313354.html

Zitter, Guy. (2016). Near death and the defibrillator: Problems and solutions for national newspapers – can advertising still be the saviour? In Mair, John, Clark, Tor, Fowler, Neil, Snoddy, Raymond, & Tait, Richard, eds. *Last Words? How Can Journalism Survive the Decline of Print?* Suffolk: Abramis Academic.

Index

Printed in the United States
by Baker & Taylor Publisher Services